THE EPIC
OUTDOOR
GRIDDLE
COOKBOOK

THE EPIC
OUTDOOR
GRIDDLE
COOKBOOK

Amazing Recipes for Griddles and Flattops

—The Waltwins—

ADAM WALTON
BRETT WALTON

Photography by Leigh Olson and Colleen Hillard

HARVARD
COMMON
PRESS

Inspiring | Educating | Creating | Entertaining

Brimming with creative inspiration, how-to projects, and useful information to enrich your everyday life, Quarto.com is a favorite destination for those pursuing their interests and passions.

© 2023 Quarto Publishing Group USA Inc.
Text © 2023 Waltwins LLC

First Published in 2023 by The Harvard Common Press, an imprint of The Quarto Group,
100 Cummings Center, Suite 265-D, Beverly, MA 01915, USA.
T (978) 282-9590 F (978) 283-2742 Quarto.com

The Harvard Common Press titles are also available at discount for retail, wholesale, promotional, and bulk purchase. For details, contact the Special Sales Manager by email at specialsales@quarto.com or by mail at The Quarto Group, Attn: Special Sales Manager, 100 Cummings Center, Suite 265-D, Beverly, MA 01915, USA.

27 26 25 24 23   1 2 3 4 5

ISBN: 978-0-7603-7817-5

Digital edition published in 2023
eISBN: 978-0-7603-7818-2

Library of Congress Cataloging-in-Publication Data available

Design and page layout: Laura Shaw Design
Cover Image: Leigh Olson Photography (recipe photos) and
    Colleen Hillary Photography (lifestyle photos)
Recipe Photography: Leigh Olson Photography
Recipe Styling: Jenelle Olson Plunkett
Lifestyle Photography: Colleen Hillard Photography

Printed in China

TO OUR KIDS, BRITTANY, ANGIE, KENZIE,
CANNON, PARKER, AND GRIFFIN.

THANK YOU FOR HELPING US
MAKE THIS LIFE TASTE BETTER.

CONTENTS

FIRE UP THE GRIDDLE!

HEY! WELCOME. We are Adam and Brett Walton, and we call ourselves the Waltwins. We want to welcome you to our backyard diner. Today's special is whatever is getting cooked up on the griddle! We have become passionate about griddle cooking and cannot wait to share that passion with you! Inside these pages, you'll become the griddle cook you've always aspired to be (or didn't know you were)! We've always said, when you're with the Waltwins, you're family! As a family, we are here to guide, teach, and show you how to hone your skills on the griddle, to become the griddle rock star in your backyard and at your next cookout! Born and raised in Utah, we loved big family cooking. Our mom, sister, and brother are among the best cooks we know, so we feel we've learned from the best! We are passing our knowledge and love on to you.

We love learning new recipes and being inventive and playful, especially when it comes to new creations on the outdoor griddle. This cold-rolled steel has become our canvas, and we know you will fall in love with these recipes. Both of us began cooking seriously on a grill, and while serving in the U.S. Army, Brett would call Adam and share his "new and favorite recipe" he just threw on the grill, which became a friendly competition—until Brett developed a keen taste for seasonings and created the Waltwins' signature Usual Suspects Seasoning (page 52) and rub. This seasoning has become a staple in many of the dishes we share on our YouTube channel—and in this book.

Our friendly competitive nature became the cornerstone for our channel, but rather than compete, we decided to share our cooks in a family-friendly way! Our dad was the king of positivity, and he instilled in us a desire to spread happiness and kindness to others. He taught us there is power in positivity and we love to share it. We feel this positivity is shared through our cooks and know that as you cook on the griddle, both the good feelings and griddle cooking will become passions for you, too. Cooking for others is a labor of love, and there is no greater feeling than cooking for so many who appreciate your skills! This feeling will continue to drive you as you become king or queen of your own backyard diner.

Within these pages, you will find 100 recipes that have the potential to become a favorite! In fact, the biggest issue you may face could be deciding what to cook next! From signature smash burgers to international favorites like fried rice, teppanyaki, and street tacos, this cookbook will carry you around the world in a culinary way that will make you an international sensation from the comfort of your backyard. You can decide which is better—the smash burger or a traditional burger. Do you prefer food from Japan or Korea? Let's find out together! Even better, this book may serve as the foundation for YOU to create your own culinary masterpieces.

We always remind our audience: We are not chefs, but we know how to make really good food. In fact, Brett may just say it best when he points out, "There are a hundred ways to get one thing done right!" And so it is with cooking—especially griddle cooking—you will find out just how amazing the whole experience is and we are here to give you the confidence to uncover your talents!

We love to cook, laugh, and share what we learn through outdoor cooking! We are here for the kid at heart and everyone else who needs a life timeout to laugh with us. We are strongest when we are together and we love being around others. Come join the fun, and remember, when you're with the Waltwins, you're family!

There are many tools we use for griddle cooking that, when used properly, help make the griddle cooking experience the ultimate cooking experience. Here is a list of the tools we use regularly and how they can be used best to help you get the most out of your griddle experience.

Dome: A basting dome is a great tool to help create steam or just raise the temperature of a specific area on a griddle. This helps when you are cooking other foods on the griddle but still need to melt the cheese on your burger. Placing the dome over the burger does not disrupt the cooking process or affect the temperature on other areas of the grill.

Large tray or bucket: Because most griddle cooks happen a bit more quickly than grill cooks do, you may find you don't have time to run into the house for something you forgot. Having a large tray or bucket to carry out all necessary items for your cook is the answer. We have several large trays, and even some bussing trays, that are ideal for this job.

Press: When we say "press," we are talking about what is known as a bacon press or grill press. There are also now specific "burger" presses. We use our presses for smash burgers, sandwiches, and even for bacon, when it's needed.

Scraper-chopper: This is our most frequently used tool. The scraper is used in nearly all of our cooks, as well as for cleaning! There's just something about holding a spatula in one hand and the scraping tool that helps give you total control of every cook! Investing in a regular scraper and a smaller food-grade "paint" scraper (wood handle slant-edge scraper) is best.

Spatulas of all sizes: We have large spatulas we use when making smash burgers or pancakes. A large spatula keeps food together when turning, moving, or flipping better than a thin, lightweight spatula will. Speaking of thinner spatulas, these are perfect, though, for a hibachi cook, or any cook where you need to keep your hands moving! Because they are lighter, your hands will be thankful that they aren't lugging the large spatula around the griddle surface.

Squeeze bottles: We have dozens of these at the house. Squeeze bottles are easy to grab and super convenient for holding different oils, sauces, and dressings. We also have one dedicated to water for steaming on the griddle.

Tongs: Just like a good spatula, the right tongs are ideal for every griddle cook. There are very few cooks we can think of when a good pair of long-handled tongs don't come in handy! The long handle is perfect for reaching over the hot griddle surface.

Warming rack: A warming rack became a bigger need than we realized it would. Because the griddle can accommodate a large amount of food at one time, we've found that a warming rack is the perfect place to move foods off direct heat while a cook is still happening. It's also the perfect place to cook biscuits right on the griddle top.

OTHER ITEMS WE LIKE TO HAVE BUT MAY NOT USE IN EVERY COOK INCLUDE:

Batter dispenser: It's hard to find a quality one, but having a batter dispenser, primarily for pancakes, is a great tool to have to make uniform pancakes that cook evenly.

Disposable grease trays: Nearly all griddle manufacturers make disposable grease trays. They are inexpensive but make the cleanup process so much easier.

Griddle soft cover: We appreciate having a hard top on our griddles, but many do not. That said, even with the hard top, the greatest way to preserve your griddle for long-term use is to have a soft water-resistant cover to protect it.

Paper towels: For a long time, I tried to use regular rags, which I would use to try to keep up with cleaning. We found, though, that having paper towels ready at all times has become extremely handy—so much so that many griddles even come with a paper towel holder now.

Shakers: When we say "shakers," we mean the larger aluminum salt and pepper (or other seasoning) shakers that can dispense larger amounts of seasoning, which can come in handy when cooking on the griddle.

Taco rack: A must-have for taco cooks! This rack also works great for holding hot dogs and sandwiches!

GRIDDLE TEMPERATURES

Cooking on a griddle is similar to cooking on a stovetop. The following temperature ranges are approximate but are what we have found, and use, through our experience. Use them to guide your cooking.

Low	250°F to 320°F	121°C to 160°C
Medium-Low	320°F to 340°F	160°C to 171°C
Medium	340°F to 410°F	171°C to 210°C
Medium-High	410°F to 430°F	210°C to 221°C
High	430°F to 500°F	221°C to 260°C

We love our outdoor griddle because we can cook entire meals on it.

SIZZLING BREAKFASTS

PERFECT SCRAMBLED EGGS

One thing that you MUST be able to cook on the griddle is scrambled eggs. Even though these are easy to do on the stovetop, we absolutely love making them on the griddle. A lot of people use milk when they make scrambled eggs, but we don't. These are the best scrambled eggs you'll ever eat—breakfast, lunch, or dinner. A garnish, like a dash of hot sauce or spoonful of salsa, makes them even better.

4 large eggs

1½ teaspoons salt

1½ teaspoons ground black pepper

1 tablespoon (14 g) unsalted butter

1. Bring the griddle to low heat.

2. In a medium-size bowl, whisk the eggs, salt, and pepper until well mixed.

3. Place the butter on the griddle to melt, spreading it out in the area where you'll cook the eggs. Slowly pour the eggs onto the griddle to make sure they don't run everywhere. As the mixture starts to cook underneath, gently fold in the sides. Continue to cook and fold the eggs for 30 to 45 seconds until fluffy and golden. Remove from the griddle and serve.

GRILLED CHEESE BREAKFAST BURRITOS

Breakfast burritos are one of our very favorites for the first meal of the day. Adding grilled cheese to the outside puts our breakfast burritos over the top. Good morning, indeed.

---

4 tablespoons (60 ml) vegetable oil, divided

6 thick-cut bacon slices

1 pound (454 g) ground mild sausage

4 to 6 large eggs

½ teaspoon salt

½ teaspoon ground black pepper

2 to 4 tablespoons (28 to 56 g) unsalted butter

1 (3-ounce, or 85 g) can Hatch green chiles

1 cup (115 g) shredded Mexican-style cheese blend

2 cups (230 g) shredded cheddar cheese

4 (10-inch, or 25 cm) burrito-size flour tortillas

Salsa for dipping

Hot sauce for dipping

1. Bring the griddle to medium-low heat. Pour 2 tablespoons (30 ml) of oil onto the griddle and let it heat until you see a wisp of white smoke.

2. Place the bacon in the hot oil and cook, turning, until crispy. Remove and chop into small bits.

3. Pour the remaining 2 tablespoons (30 ml) of oil onto the griddle and place the sausage on top. Cook the sausage until browned and no longer pink, then remove from the griddle.

4. In a medium-size bowl, whisk the eggs, salt, and pepper to combine.

5. Place the butter on the griddle to melt, spreading it out in the area where you'll cook the eggs. Slowly pour the eggs onto the griddle to make sure they don't run everywhere. As the mixture starts to cook underneath, gently fold in the sides. Continue to cook and fold the eggs for 30 to 45 seconds until fluffy and golden.

6. Pour the can of green chiles onto the eggs, add the bacon, sausage, and Mexican-style cheese blend. Cook, mixing it all together, until the cheese melts. Transfer the egg mixture to a large bowl or plate.

7. Place one tortilla on a clean work surface. Place a large spoonful of the eggs in the middle of the tortilla. Fold in the sides first, then from the edge closest to you, pull the tortilla over the ingredients and finish rolling the burrito. Repeat with the remaining tortillas and eggs.

8. Lay down a strip of shredded cheddar on the griddle, the length of a burrito, and place the first burrito directly onto the cheese. Cook for 30 to 45 seconds, then place another strip of shredded cheddar directly in front of the burrito. Using a scraper or spatula, start to roll the burrito from the back, making sure the cheese sticks to the tortilla, and roll it onto the front strip of cheddar. Cook for 30 to 45 seconds, then carefully pull the burrito off the griddle, making sure the cheese is stuck to the tortilla and repeat this process with each burrito. Serve with salsa and hot sauce for dipping.

BREAKFAST CREPES

Adam first made crepes in seventh-grade home economics class. The light and fluffy flavor and texture are unforgettable, and the ease with which these cook on the griddle makes them a no-brainer for breakfast. Serve with your favorite fillings, such as fresh bananas, blueberries, raspberries, or strawberries, and top with a drizzle of caramel sauce, chocolate syrup, or honey, and a dusting of powdered sugar.

1 cup (120 g) all-purpose flour

¾ cup (180 ml) whole milk

½ cup (120 ml) water

3 tablespoons (45 ml) melted unsalted butter, plus more for cooking

2 large eggs

1 tablespoon (12.5 g) sugar

1½ teaspoons vanilla extract

Pinch of salt

Filling of choice for serving

1. In a medium-size bowl, whisk the flour, milk, water, melted butter, eggs, sugar, vanilla, and salt until smooth. Cover and refrigerate for at least 1 hour.

2. Bring the griddle to medium heat.

3. Place 1 tablespoon (14 g) of butter on the griddle to melt. Pour one ladleful of batter onto the melted butter, then use a clean dowel, in a circular motion, to flatten the batter. Once flat, lift and flip the crepe to cook the second side—no more than 30 seconds per side. Repeat with the remaining batter, adding more butter as needed.

4. To fill the crepes: Place the crepes on a work surface. Put your filling into the center of the crepe and gently fold each side over the filling.

EGGNOG FRENCH TOAST

MAKES 4 SLICES FRENCH TOAST

If you are looking for a holiday tradition, may we suggest this eggnog French toast? This is Adam's son Parker's favorite meal prepared on the griddle. Serve with your favorite toppings.

1 cup (240 ml) eggnog

2 large eggs

1 tablespoon (14 g) unsalted butter

4 slices artisan bread (such as brioche)

1. In a shallow bowl, whisk the eggnog and eggs until fully combined.

2. Bring the griddle to medium-low heat.

3. Place the butter on the griddle to melt. One at a time, dredge the bread slices in the eggnog wash and place it in the melted butter. Cook for 1 to 2 minutes until browning begins. Flip the bread and cook for 1 to 2 minutes more, or until browned.

APPETIZERS, SIDES & SWEET TREATS

CRISPY FRIED GREEN TOMATOES

There's almost nothing more Southern than fried green tomatoes. This recipe creates a refreshing, lightly fried snack that will have your friends and family speaking with a Southern accent (if they don't already!). Serve with your favorite dipping sauce, like our Fry Sauce (page 92).

---

1 cup (115 g) breadcrumbs

1 cup (140 g) cornmeal

2 tablespoons (24 g) Waltwins Usual
    Suspects Seasoning, divided (page 52)

1 or 2 cups (240 to 480 ml) buttermilk

2 cups (240 g) all-purpose flour

3 or 4 large green tomatoes, cut into
    ¼- to ½-inch (0.6 to 1 cm)-thick slices

½ cup (120 ml) vegetable oil

1. In a shallow bowl, whisk the breadcrumbs, cornmeal, and 1 tablespoon (12 g) of Usual Suspects Seasoning to combine. Pour the buttermilk into another shallow bowl and place the flour in a third shallow bowl.

2. Season the tomatoes with the remaining 1 tablespoon (12 g) of Usual Suspects Seasoning. Coat the seasoned tomato slices in the flour, then dredge in the buttermilk, and finally in the breadcrumb-cornmeal mixture, completely coating the slices.

3. Bring the griddle to medium-low to medium heat.

4. Pour the oil onto the griddle to create a shallow-fry area. Let heat until you see a wisp of white smoke.

5. Place the coated tomatoes in the hot oil and cook for about 1 minute until the bottoms begin to turn golden brown. Flip the tomatoes and cook on the second side for about 1 minute until golden brown. Pull the tomatoes off the griddle and let cool for 2 to 3 minutes before serving.

POUTINE

Brett gets all of the credit for this delicious dish. He repeatedly pushed Adam to just give this savory Canadian favorite a try—and the rest is history! It combines so many of our favorite things in the most scrumptious way.

1 large russet potato, cut lengthwise into fries

1 cup (240 ml) water, plus more for soaking

4 tablespoons (60 ml) peanut oil

1 tablespoon (18 g) salt

1 (0.87-ounce, or 24 g) package brown gravy mix

1 cup (240 ml) water

1 (16-ounce, or 454 g) package cheese curds

1. In a large bowl, combine the fries and enough water to cover. Let soak for 5 to 10 minutes.

2. Bring one side of the griddle to medium-low heat and the other side to medium-high heat.

3. Remove the fries from the water and lay flat on a paper towel. Cover with another paper towel and pat dry.

4. Pour 2 tablespoons (30 ml) of oil onto the cooler side of the griddle, letting it settle to create a "griddle fry." Place half of the fries flat in the hot oil. Cook for 7 to 10 minutes until they start to turn light brown, then remove from the griddle and let rest for 2 minutes. Repeat, cooking the remaining fries until they turn light brown, then removing them to rest for 2 minutes.

5. Pour 2 tablespoons (30 ml) of oil onto the hotter side of the griddle and place the first batch of fries in the oil. Cook for 5 to 7 minutes until they are GBD (golden, brown, and delicious), then pull them off the griddle and season with salt. Repeat with the second batch of fries.

6. Place a small pot over high heat and pour in the contents of the gravy packet. While stirring, slowly pour in the water. Cook until the gravy starts to boil, stir well, then pull the pan off the griddle.

7. Plate half of the fries. Put one small handful of cheese curds on top of the fries, then put the rest of the fries on top of the cheese and top them with one more small handful of cheese curds. Slowly pour the gravy over the top and enjoy!

CHEESESTEAK EGG ROLLS

MAKES 8 TO 10 MEDIUM-SIZE EGG ROLLS

Want to impress your family and friends with what might be the "star" appetizer at the next big gathering? This. Is. IT! The first time we made these, we were lucky to get a bite because they were devoured within seconds. This recipe may need to be doubled, or even tripled, to satisfy the crowd.

6 to 8 tablespoons (90 to 120 ml) vegetable oil, divided

2 tablespoons (28 g) unsalted butter

1 large yellow onion, diced

1 green bell pepper, diced

2 teaspoons salt, divided

2 teaspoons ground black pepper, divided

1 pound (454 g) rib eye, shaved or as thinly sliced as possible

8 to 10 egg roll wrappers

10 slices provolone cheese

½ cup (120 ml) water

Favorite dipping sauce for serving

1. Bring the griddle to medium-low heat.

2. Pour 1 tablespoon (15 ml) of oil onto the griddle, then place the butter in it to melt. Lay the onion in the melted butter, followed by the green pepper and add 1 teaspoon of salt and 1 teaspoon of pepper. Cook for 5 to 6 minutes, moving the vegetables slowly, until the onion begins to turn translucent. Move the vegetables to a cooler side of the griddle, not over direct heat, or set aside off the griddle.

3. Pour 3 to 4 tablespoons (45 to 60 ml) of oil onto the griddle. Place the rib eye flat in the hot oil, spreading it out, and season with the remaining 1 teaspoon of salt and 1 teaspoon of pepper. Cook for 1 to 2 minutes to create a sear. Once the meat begins to turn brown, indicating it is cooking through, stir and chop the rib eye with a scraper to break up the meat. Mix in the onion and pepper and set aside.

4. Place 1 egg roll wrapper on a work surface in a "diamond" shape, with one corner aimed down (this helps with the rolling and folding process). In the middle of the wrapper, place a spoonful of the steak and vegetables, then place 1 slice of provolone over the steak, folding it to fit. Fold the bottom corner of the egg roll wrapper up and over the meat and cheese, then fold in each side of the wrapper, tucking them tightly while not breaking the wrapper. Once the sides are folded (like an envelope), continue to roll the egg roll, leaving just the top inch exposed. Dip your finger in the water and run it along the exposed edge of the wrapper to help "seal" the egg roll. Repeat with the remaining ingredients.

5. If needed, pour the remaining 2 to 3 tablespoons (30 to 45 ml) of oil onto the griddle and place the egg rolls in the oil. Cook for 1 to 2 minutes until the bottoms are golden brown. Flip each egg roll and continue to cook, turning as necessary, until all sides are golden brown. If the ends need to be crisped, hold the egg rolls with tongs so they stand on end. Pull the egg rolls off the griddle and slice diagonally from one corner to the other. Serve with your favorite dipping sauce.

RUSSIAN DRESSING

MAKES SCANT 1 CUP (240 G)

Do you want to impress your family and guests? Make this amazing-tasting Russian dressing that is a true crowd-pleaser—and tastes just like it came straight out of a Chicago deli!

½ cup (120 g) mayonnaise

3 tablespoons (45 g) ketchup

2 tablespoons (30 g) horseradish

2 teaspoons Worcestershire sauce

1 tablespoon (12.5 g) sugar

¼ teaspoon paprika

1 medium-size dill pickle, diced

Salt and ground black pepper

In a medium-size bowl, whisk the mayo, ketchup, horseradish, Worcestershire sauce, sugar, paprika, and pickle until blended and thick. Taste and season with salt and pepper, as needed.

THREE-INGREDIENT QUESO BLANCO

SERVES 6 TO 8

We've got to admit, we never imagined these three simple ingredients (plus one optional ingredient that's not necessary for the dip to taste amazing) would come together so perfectly, and yet, here we are. This simple queso blanco is a quick go-to favorite any time we break out the chips.

1 pound (454 g) white American cheese (block of cheese from the deli)

½ cup (120 ml) whole milk

1 (4-ounce, or 115 g) can diced green chilies

½ teaspoon sodium citrate (optional)

1. Bring the griddle to high heat.

2. While the griddle heats up, cut the cheese into roughly 1-inch (2.5 cm) cubes.

3. Once the griddle is hot, place a medium-size pot on it. Place the cheese in the pot and pour in the milk, chilies, and sodium citrate (if using). Cook, stirring occasionally, until the cheese is melted. Let cool a bit before dipping in.

MEXICAN STREET CORN (ELOTES)

SERVES 8

Yes, it really tastes as good as it looks! The smoky chipotle pepper brings all the flavors together, making you wonder why you ever ate corn on the cob any other way.

½ cup (120 g) Mexican crema

½ cup (120 g) mayonnaise

½ cup (8 g) minced fresh cilantro

2 tablespoons (30 ml) freshly squeezed lime juice

2 teaspoons grated lime zest

1 garlic clove, minced

8 medium-size ears sweet corn, husked

2 tablespoons (30 ml) vegetable oil

½ cup (60 g) crumbled Cotija cheese

1 teaspoon ground chipotle pepper

1. In a medium-size bowl, whisk the crema, mayo, cilantro, lime juice, lime zest, and garlic until blended. Refrigerate until needed.

2. Bring the griddle to medium-low heat.

3. Pour the oil onto the griddle and place the corn in the oil. Cook the corn for 15 to 20 minutes, rotating it every 2 minutes to ensure it does not burn, and cooking until your desired doneness is achieved (medium-brown color on the softened corn kernels. (Alternatively, add 2 to 3 tablespoons, or 30 to 45 ml, of water, close the hood or place a dome on the corn, and steam for about 15 minutes, turning the corn every 2 minutes, until done.)

4. Pull the corn off the griddle and let cool for 3 minutes. Using a basting brush or a spoon, lather each ear of corn entirely with the crema mixture. Sprinkle all sides with Cotija cheese and season with chipotle pepper to taste.

FRIED PICKLE CHIPS

SERVES 6 TO 8

In the words of Adam's wife, Jen, "You've ruined getting fried pickles as an appetizer" every time we eat out! These homemade fried pickles really are as good, if not better, than any we've had anywhere. Serve with your favorite dipping sauce, like our Fry Sauce (page 92)!

1 (32-ounce, or 905 g) jar dill hamburger pickle chips

2 cups (240 g) all-purpose flour

1 to 2 tablespoons (12 to 24 g) Waltwins Usual Suspects Seasoning (page 52)

1 to 2 teaspoons paprika

2 cups (480 ml) buttermilk

2 to 3 tablespoons (30 to 45 ml) vegetable oil

1. Pour the pickles into a colander in the sink to drain. Rinse with cold water, drain again, and pat dry with paper towels.

2. In a large bowl, whisk the flour, Usual Suspects Seasoning to taste, and paprika to taste. Pour the buttermilk into a shallow bowl. One by one, coat each pickle chip in the flour mixture, dip it into the buttermilk, then back into the flour mixture to coat completely. Place the coated pickles on a plate, then bring the plate to the griddle.

3. Bring the griddle to medium-low heat.

4. Pour the oil onto the griddle and let heat until you see a wisp of white smoke. Place the coated pickles in the shallow-fry oil and cook for 3 to 4 minutes until the bottoms begin to turn golden brown. Flip the pickles and cook for 3 to 4 minutes until the second side is also golden brown. Pull the pickles off the griddle and let cool for 2 to 3 minutes before serving.

PINEAPPLE COLESLAW

The perfect bed for Coconut Shrimp (page 158) tacos, at least, that's what we use this recipe for, and we have to say, we can't imagine making coconut shrimp tacos without it!

1 (12-ounce, or 340 g) bag broccoli
    slaw mix

½ pineapple, trimmed, peeled, cored,
    and diced, juice reserved

1 cup (240 g) mayonnaise

1 tablespoon (15 ml) rice vinegar

1 teaspoon ground white pepper

½ teaspoon salt

1. In a large bowl, combine the broccoli slaw and pineapple.

2. In a small bowl, whisk the mayonnaise, vinegar, reserved pineapple juice, white pepper, and salt until smooth. Pour the sauce over the broccoli mixture and toss to coat evenly. Refrigerate for 4 to 6 hours, or overnight for the best flavor. Toss before serving.

HAWAIIAN MACARONI SALAD

No Hawaiian plate lunch is complete without the amazing macaroni salad and white rice on the side! As the perfect side dish with Hawaiian Barbecue Chicken (page 79), or as a stand-alone meal, this salad is perfection!

---

1 pound (454 g) elbow macaroni

6 tablespoons (90 ml) apple cider vinegar

3 teaspoons (18 g) kosher salt, divided

1 cup (240 ml) whole milk, plus more
    as needed

6 tablespoons (75 g) sugar

2 cups (480 g) mayonnaise, divided

½ cup (80 g) grated or minced white onion

2 cups (220 g) grated carrot

1 teaspoon ground white pepper

4 scallions, white and green parts,
    thinly sliced

1. Cook the macaroni according to the package directions. Drain and transfer to a large bowl. While the pasta is still hot, stir in the vinegar and set aside to cool.

2. In a small bowl, stir together 1½ teaspoons (9 g) of salt, the milk, sugar, and 1 cup (240 g) of mayonnaise until blended. Add the mayo mixture to the still slightly warm macaroni and mix until well coated. Cover and refrigerate for 1 hour, or up to 4 hours, until fully cooled.

3. To the cooled macaroni, add the remaining 1 cup (240 g) of mayonnaise, the onion, and carrot. Gently stir to coat and combine. If the pasta appears a bit dry, add up to ½ cup (120 ml) more milk. Season with the remaining 1½ teaspoons (9 g) of salt and the white pepper. Garnish with the scallions to serve.

STATE FAIR FUNNEL CAKES

MAKES 8 TO 10 LARGE FUNNEL CAKES

Oh, how we LOVE our fair foods, and this recipe is definitely worthy of a blue ribbon! These cakes were a breeze once we discovered how to use an aluminum pan on the griddle surface safely.

Vegetable oil for frying

1 cup (240 ml) milk

2 large eggs

2 tablespoons (25 g) granulated sugar

1 teaspoon vanilla extract

2 cups (240 g) all-purpose flour

1 teaspoon baking powder

¼ teaspoon salt

Powdered sugar for sprinkling

1. Bring the griddle to medium-high heat.

2. Place a 15.75 × 11.25-inch (39 × 28 cm) aluminum foil pan on the griddle and fill it with about 2 inches (5 cm) of oil. Bring the oil to between 365°F and 375°F (185°C and 190.5°C).

3. While the oil comes to temperature, in a large bowl, whisk the milk, eggs, granulated sugar, and vanilla until well mixed. In a medium-size bowl, whisk the flour, baking powder, and salt to combine. Add the dry ingredients to the wet ingredients and whisk until evenly mixed with no clumps. Transfer the batter to a pouring pitcher, or use a plastic bag with a small to medium-size hole cut out of a bottom corner (keep the hole covered until you are ready to pour the batter into the oil).

4. In a circular motion, pour the batter into the hot oil, ensuring the batter lays over itself as it cooks, forming a 6-inch (15 cm) cake. Fry the cake for 1 to 2 minutes until golden brown. Flip the cake and cook for 1 to 2 minutes until the second side is golden brown. Transfer the funnel cake to a paper towel to drain. Sprinkle with powdered sugar while hot and serve. Repeat with the remaining batter.

CHOCOLATE CHIP GRIDDLE COOKIES

MAKES ABOUT 4 DOZEN COOKIES

This recipe is the only one our family uses for chocolate chip cookies. We cannot argue whether this may be better cooked in the oven, but we can say that when camping, tailgating, or otherwise with no access to an oven, this method works perfectly.

---

1 cup (200 g) granulated sugar

1 cup (225 g) packed light brown sugar

1½ teaspoons vanilla extract

2 large eggs

1 cup (2 sticks, or 224 g) unsalted butter, at room temperature, plus more for the griddle

½ teaspoon salt

½ teaspoon baking powder

3 cups (360 g) all-purpose flour

2 cups (350 g) chocolate chips (we use milk chocolate, but use your preference)

1. In a large bowl, combine the granulated sugar, brown sugar, vanilla, eggs, and butter. Using a handheld mixer, mix on low speed until the ingredients are evenly mixed. Add the salt, baking powder, and flour, mixing well. Add the chocolate chips and mix for 15 seconds. Scoop the dough into small balls.

2. Bring one side of the griddle to medium-low heat.

3. We're using indirect heat to cook the cookies, so place 1 tablespoon (14 g) of butter on the cooler side of the griddle (the side not turned on) to melt. Place the cookie balls on the buttered griddle surface, ensuring there is space between them so they do not cook together. Cook for about 12 minutes until the edges begin to brown and the centers appear set and begin to lose their sheen. Remove and let cool.

4. To bake in the oven: Preheat the oven to 375°F (190°C or gas mark 5). Place the cookies on a baking sheet and bake for 9 minutes (when you pull them out of the oven, they will still be soft). Transfer to a paper towel for 10 minutes to cool and harden some. Enjoy!

OUR FAVORITE GUACAMOLE

MAKES ABOUT 2 CUPS (450 G)

Just like everything we make, we couldn't wait to perfect the art of guacamole! We aren't saying others out there aren't better than this one; we're just saying we haven't found one yet that is. Serve with your favorite tortilla chips for dipping.

½ red onion, diced

2 Roma tomatoes, diced

3 tablespoons (3 g) chopped fresh cilantro

2 garlic cloves, minced

3 avocados

½ teaspoon sea salt, plus more as needed

2 tablespoons (30 ml) freshly squeezed lime juice, plus more as needed

1. In a large bowl, combine the onion, tomatoes, cilantro, and garlic.

2. Halve the avocados and remove the pits. Scoop the avocado flesh into the bowl with the other ingredients. Add the salt and lime juice. Using a fork, mix all the ingredients, mashing the avocado during the process. (The key is to mash most of the avocado, while preserving some "chunks" for texture and taste.) Taste and add more salt or lime juice, as needed.

CHICKEN EVERY WHICH WAY

CHEESY CHICKEN PIZZAIOLA

Adam learned this simple recipe from his wife and it fast became a family favorite. The seasoning makes about ¼ cup (about 50 g) for a shaker and will keep, stored in a cool, dry place, for up to 6 months.

FOR WALTWINS USUAL SUSPECTS SEASONING:

1 tablespoon (18 g) salt

1 tablespoon (10 g) garlic powder

1 tablespoon (12 g) Ac´cent Flavor Enhancer

1½ teaspoons ground black pepper

1½ teaspoons onion powder

1½ teaspoons adobo seasoning

FOR CHEESY CHICKEN PIZZAIOLA:

1 (24-ounce, or 70 ml) jar marinara sauce

1 (16-ounce, or 454 g) package penne pasta

1 to 2 tablespoons (15 to 30 ml) vegetable or olive oil

4 boneless, skinless chicken breasts, pounded thin

4 ounces (115 g) thinly sliced deli ham, or enough to cover each chicken breast with 2 or 3 slices

Shredded mozzarella cheese for topping

1. To make the Usual Suspects Seasoning: In a small bowl, stir together all the Usual Suspects ingredients, then transfer to a shaker.

2. To make the chicken pizzaiola: In a small saucepan over medium heat, warm the marinara sauce. Keep warm until serving.

3. While the sauce warms, bring a large pot full of water to a boil. Add the pasta and cook according to the package instructions. Drain and set aside while you prepare the main dish.

4. Preheat the griddle to medium-low heat.

5. Coat the hot griddle with oil, place the chicken on it, and season liberally with Usual Suspects Seasoning. Cook for 3 to 4 minutes, flip the chicken, and cook for 3 to 4 minutes more. Continue cooking and flipping until the internal temperature of the chicken reaches a minimum of 165°F (74°C), 8 to 10 minutes total. Move the chicken to the cooler side of the griddle, not over direct heat.

6. Place the ham slices on the griddle and cook for 20 to 30 seconds, just long enough to get them hot. Pull the ham off the griddle.

7. Place the pasta and three-fourths of the sauce in a large serving dish. Toss to coat.

8. Turn the griddle to low heat and move the chicken over direct heat. Top each piece with a generous spoonful of the remaining sauce, then with two or three slices of ham. Sprinkle with mozzarella to taste. Dome the chicken to melt the cheese. Transfer the chicken to the serving dish with the pasta and sauce. If you like it saucy, spread the remaining sauce over the entire dish before serving.

COUNTRY-STYLE CHICKEN-FRIED CHICKEN

SERVES 2 TO 4

While chicken-fried steak is a personal favorite of Brett's, Adam prefers the chicken version. The process is the same, but the juicy, tender nature of the fried chicken makes this a hard-to-beat taste at home.

3 to 5 tablespoons (45 to 75 ml) vegetable oil

2 cups (240 g) all-purpose flour

4 teaspoons (24 g) salt, divided

4 teaspoons (8 g) ground black pepper, divided

1 tablespoon (14 g) seasoning salt

2 cups (480 ml) buttermilk

2 large boneless, skinless chicken breasts

1. Bring the griddle to medium-low heat.

2. Pour the oil onto the griddle to create a shallow-fry area.

3. While the oil heats, in a shallow bowl, thoroughly stir together the flour, 3 teaspoons (18 g) of salt, 3 teaspoons (6 g) of pepper, and the seasoning salt. Pour the buttermilk into another shallow bowl.

4. Pound the chicken flat to tenderize it and help it cook quickly and evenly. Season with the remaining 1 teaspoon of salt and 1 teaspoon of pepper. Dredge the chicken pieces in the flour mix, coating the entire piece and pressing the flour into the chicken to ensure complete coverage. Dredge the chicken in the buttermilk until completely covered, and then dredge it in the flour again, ensuring complete coverage. Lay the chicken on the griddle in the hot oil. Watching carefully to ensure the breading does not burn, cook the chicken, flipping it every 2 minutes, until each side is golden brown and the internal temperature reaches 165°F (74°C).

SESAME CHICKEN

Sesame chicken may just be the most popular dish ordered in any Asian restaurant. This at-home recipe brings the same flavors to your griddle, and you'll love being able to make this takeout favorite at home in less time and serve with your favorite sides.

FOR CHICKEN:

1 large egg

1 tablespoon (8 g) cornstarch

3 tablespoons (23 g) all-purpose flour

1 teaspoon salt

1 teaspoon Ac'cent Flavor Enhancer

½ teaspoon ground black pepper

2 pounds (908 g) boneless, skinless chicken breast, cut into 1-inch (2.5 cm) pieces

FOR SAUCE:

½ cup (120 g) ketchup

⅓ cup (80 ml) soy sauce (reduced-sodium if possible)

¼ cup (80 g) honey

3 tablespoons (43 g) brown sugar

2 tablespoons (30 ml) rice vinegar

1 tablespoon (15 ml) toasted sesame oil

½ cup (120 ml) water

2 teaspoons cornstarch

FOR FINISHING:

3 tablespoons (45 ml), 1 teaspoon vegetable oil, divided

1 teaspoon minced garlic

2 tablespoons (16 g) sesame seeds

2 tablespoons (12 g) sliced scallion, white and green parts

1. Bring one side of the griddle to high heat.

2. To make the chicken: While the griddle heats, in a large bowl, whisk the egg, flour, cornstarch, salt, Ac'cent, and pepper to combine. Add the chicken and mix well to coat. Set aside.

3. To make the sauce. In a medium-size bowl, whisk the ketchup, soy sauce, honey, brown sugar, rice vinegar, and sesame oil to combine.

4. To finish: Place a wok or large skillet on the hot griddle surface. Pour in 1 teaspoon of vegetable oil and add the garlic. Stir-fry for about 30 seconds until fragrant—do not let the garlic burn. Stir in the sauce and bring to a boil. In a small bowl, whisk the water and cornstarch until the cornstarch dissolves. Whisk this slurry into the boiling sauce and return the sauce to a rolling boil, whisking occasionally. Reduce the heat to medium and cook the sauce until it reaches your desired thickness, then turn off the heat.

5. While the sauce cooks, bring a separate part of the griddle to medium-low heat.

6. Pour 3 tablespoons (45 ml) of vegetable oil onto the hot griddle and lay the chicken in the oil. Stir-fry the chicken for 6 to 10 minutes, or until cooked thoroughly and no longer pink. Transfer the chicken to paper towels to drain. Add the chicken to the sauce. Serve garnished with sesame seeds and scallion.

FIERY TORTILLA-CRUSTED CHICKEN NUGGETS

It didn't take long for Adam to learn about Takis Fuego spicy rolled tortilla chips as a middle school teacher. In fact, this dish was a student-requested cook that we were all too happy to honor. These nuggets bring a different kick we absolutely love. And a side of ranch or blue cheese for dipping is definitely recommended.

---

1 (9.9-ounce, or 281 g) bag Takis Fuego rolled tortilla chips

1 cup (120 g) all-purpose flour

1 cup (240 ml) buttermilk

1 pound (454 g) boneless, skinless chicken breast, cut into 1-inch (2.5 cm) pieces

4 to 5 tablespoons (60 to 75 ml) vegetable oil

1. Place the tortilla chips in a large resealable plastic bag, seal the bag, and smash the chips until they are small crumbs (alternatively, do this in a food processor).

2. Bring the griddle to medium to medium-high heat.

3. Put the flour into a medium-size shallow bowl. Pour the buttermilk into another shallow bowl and place the tortilla crumbs in a third bowl. One at a time, dredge the chicken pieces in the flour to cover completely, then submerge in the buttermilk to cover and coat, then place the nuggets in the tortilla crumbs, ensuring each piece is fully coated.

4. Pour 3 to 4 tablespoons (45 to 60 ml) of oil onto the griddle, creating a shallow-fry area, and let heat until you see a wisp of white smoke.

5. Carefully place each chicken nugget in the hot oil. Cook for about 1 minute until the bottom begins to darken in color. Flip the nuggets and repeat the process, cooking for about 1 minute and adding more oil as needed, on all sides until each is darkened. Pull the nuggets off the griddle and set aside to cool slightly before serving.

BARBECUE CHICKEN WINGS

Are you in the mood for wings, but not for the heat and spice? These barbecue chicken wings will satisfy that hankering in such a delectable way. Wings can be the perfect vessel for your favorite barbecue sauce.

4½ pounds (2 kg) chicken wings

¼ cup (about 1 recipe, or 48 g) Waltwins Usual Suspects Seasoning (page 52)

3 tablespoons (45 ml) vegetable oil

1 to 1½ cups (250 to 375 g) favorite barbecue sauce

1. Put the wings in a large bowl or pot and sprinkle the Usual Suspects Seasoning over them. Stir or toss to coat the wings and distribute the seasoning evenly.

2. Bring the griddle to medium-low heat.

3. Pour about 3 tablespoons (45 m) of oil onto the griddle. Lay the wings in the oil and cook for 20 to 30 minutes (larger wings can take up to 45 minutes), turning them constantly to keep from burning, until the wings are crispy and the internal temperature reaches a minimum of 165°F (74°C). If you want to cook the wings longer, we find that wings cooked above 180°F (82°C) were much crispier (some even reached 200°F, or 93°C; cooking about 10 minutes more).

4. Baste the cooked wings with your favorite barbecue sauce, covering them liberally, and cook, turning, until the sauce begins to crisp. Pull and serve.

SWEET STICKY BUFFALO SANDWICHES

SERVES 2

Looking for a creative way to change up your buffalo chicken game? We've got you covered. We learned this sticky buffalo recipe many years ago and it's been a favorite ever since. The sauce can be used for all things chicken-fried! Note: The aluminum pan used for frying is thin and punctures easily. We recommend adding the oil while the pan is on the griddle, and avoid using knives or tongs in the pan.

FOR SWEET STICKY BUFFALO SAUCE:

1½ cups (338 g) packed light brown sugar

6 tablespoons (90 ml) Frank's RedHot Original Cayenne Pepper Sauce

¼ cup (60 ml) water

FOR SWEET STICKY BUFFALO SANDWICH:

Vegetable oil for frying

2 to 3 cups (240 to 360 g) all-purpose flour

Salt and ground black pepper

1 cup (240 ml) buttermilk

1 large boneless, skinless chicken breast, halved horizontally

2 kaiser rolls, split

Mayonnaise for serving

Ranch or blue cheese dressing for serving

Sandwich pickles for serving

1. To make the buffalo sauce: In a medium-size saucepan over medium-low heat on the stovetop or griddle, whisk the brown sugar, hot sauce, and water to combine. Cook, stirring occasionally, until the brown sugar is dissolved. Set aside for dipping and basting.

2. To make the buffalo sandwich: Bring the griddle to medium-high heat.

3. Place a 15.75 × 11.25-inch (39 × 28 cm) aluminum foil pan on the griddle over high heat and fill it half full of oil. Bring the oil to between 325°F and 345°F (163°C and 174°C). If it gets hotter than this, bring the temperature down. You do not want to burn the breading on the chicken before the meat is cooked through.

4. Place the flour in a shallow bowl and season with salt and pepper. Whisk to combine. Place the buttermilk in another shallow bowl. One piece at a time, coat the chicken in the buttermilk, then dredge in the seasoned flour, ensuring the entire breast is covered (including any cracks; it helps to press the flour into the chicken). Shake off any excess flour and gently place the chicken in the hot oil. Fry for 1 to 2 minutes, flip the chicken, and cook until the breading is a light golden brown color (it will continue to darken after being pulled from the oil). Check the internal temperature of the chicken to ensure it is at least 165°F (74°C). Baste the hot chicken with the sticky buffalo sauce.

5. To build the sandwiches: Put the rolls on plates, cut-side up, and spread both halves with mayo. Top the bottom bun with a piece of chicken, then a dab of ranch, some pickle slices, and finish with the top bun. Pass the extra sauce for dipping.

NASHVILLE HOT CHICKEN SANDWICHES

Until you've had a Nashville hot chicken sandwich, you just don't know! This recipe delivered on such a high level that it became an instant memory that we still talk about: "Remember the first time we made those Nashville hot chicken sandwiches?" one of us will say, to which the response is always: "How could I forget?!"

FOR BRINE:

2 to 3 cups (480 to 720 ml) buttermilk

1 cup (240 ml) pickle brine

Waltwins Usual Suspects Seasoning (page 52) for seasoning

2 boneless, skinless chicken thighs

FOR SAUCE:

2 tablespoons (10 g) cayenne pepper

1½ tablespoons (23 g) brown sugar, plus more as needed

½ teaspoon chili powder

½ teaspoon garlic powder

½ cup (120 ml) vegetable oil

FOR DREDGE:

2 cups (240 g) all-purpose flour

2 tablespoons (24 g) Waltwins Usual Suspects Seasoning (page 52)

1 tablespoon (7 g) paprika

2 to 3 teaspoons vegetable oil

Mayonnaise for serving

Kaiser rolls for serving

Sandwich pickles for serving (preferably Claussen)

1. To make the brine: In a shallow dish, whisk the buttermilk, pickle brine, and Usual Suspects Seasoning to taste until blended. Add the chicken thighs and turn them to coat in the brine. Cover and refrigerate for at least 1 hour, or up to 3 hours.

2. To make the sauce: While the chicken marinates, in a small bowl, whisk the sauce ingredients to combine and set aside. The sauce may separate, so whisk again occasionally.

3. To make the dredge: In a shallow bowl, stir together the flour, Usual Suspects Seasoning, and paprika to blend.

4. Bring the griddle to medium-low heat.

5. Pour 2 to 3 tablespoons (30 to 45 ml) of oil onto the griddle and let heat until you see a wisp of white smoke. Remove the chicken from the brine and dredge it in the flour mix to completely coat, then place the chicken in the hot oil. Discard the brine. Cook for about 2 minutes, or until the bottom side is golden brown. Flip the chicken and cook the other side for about 2 minutes until golden brown. Continue flipping and cooking the chicken until the internal temperature reaches at least 165°F (74°C).

6. Pull the cooked chicken off the griddle and place it on paper towels or a cooling rack to drain. Whisk the sauce and coat the chicken with it, ensuring full coverage.

7. To assemble: Spread mayo on the cut sides of the rolls. Place a piece of chicken on the bottom roll, top with two pickle slices, and add the top roll.

CHICKEN "CHEESESTEAK" SANDWICHES

Not a fan of beef cheesesteak? Try these chicken cheesesteaks. They're so good, you may be more apt to choose chicken over rib eye for your next sandwich.

---

3 tablespoons (45 ml) vegetable oil

3 tablespoons (42 g) unsalted butter

1 large yellow onion, diced

1 pound (454 g) chicken breast, cut into
    1-inch (2.5 cm) cubes

Salt and ground black pepper

12 slices provolone cheese

4 hoagie rolls, split horizontally

1. Bring the griddle to medium-low heat.

2. Pour 1 tablespoon (15 ml) of oil onto the griddle, then add the butter to melt. Lay the onion in the melted butter and season with 1 teaspoon of salt and 1 teaspoon of pepper. Cook for 5 to 6 minutes, moving the onion slowly, until it begins to turn translucent. Move the onion to a cooler side of the griddle, not over direct heat, or take it off the griddle.

3. Pour the remaining 2 tablespoons (30 ml) of oil onto the griddle and lay the chicken in the oil. Season with salt and pepper to taste. Cook the chicken, slowly stirring it, until it turns golden brown and is no longer pink. Stir and "chop" the chicken with a scraper to break it into smaller pieces. Mix in the onion, then divide the chicken and onion into four even lines, each the length of a hoagie roll. Lay three slices of cheese on each line of chicken to melt.

4. Place the hoagie rolls on the griddle for about 1 minute to warm the outside of each roll. Open each roll and place one facedown on each line of chicken and let sit for about 30 seconds. Using a spatula, scoop up the chicken cheesesteak, holding firm to the hoagie, and turn the whole sandwich right-side up.

CHICKEN BACON RANCH SANDWICHES

SERVES 2

It may not get simpler than this, but simple is often the best way to accomplish greatness, and this sandwich is great. If you love ranch, you will love this sandwich.

---

1 (1-ounce, or 28 g) packet ranch
    dressing mix

1 cup (240 ml) milk

1 cup (240 g) mayonnaise

3 bacon slices, halved widthwise

2 boneless, skinless chicken breast cutlets

Waltwins Usual Suspects Seasoning
    (page 52) for seasoning

2 tablespoons (30 ml) vegetable oil

2 ciabatta rolls, halved horizontally

Mayonnaise for toasting the rolls

2 slices Swiss cheese

1 avocado, peeled, halved, pitted,
    and cut into slices

1 large tomato, cut into slices

1. In a small bowl, whisk the ranch dressing mix, milk, and mayo to blend. Cover and refrigerate until needed.

2. Bring the griddle to medium-low heat.

3. While coming to temperature, place the bacon on the griddle and cook to your desired crispness.

4. While the bacon cooks, season the chicken liberally with the Usual Suspects Seasoning.

5. Pour the oil onto the griddle and place the chicken in it. Cook for 4 minutes. Flip the chicken and cook for 3 minutes more, or until the internal temperature reaches 165°F (74°C). If you are using a larger chicken breast, you may need to repeat flipping to avoid burning the chicken until it comes to the correct food-safe temperature.

6. Pull the cooked bacon and chicken off the griddle and let the chicken rest for 5 minutes before serving.

7. While the chicken rests, spread mayonnaise on the cut sides of the rolls and place the rolls facedown on the griddle. Cook until the rolls begin to crisp and turn a golden brown. Pull the rolls off the griddle and build your sandwich! We recommend: bottom roll, layer of ranch dressing, chicken cutlet, Swiss cheese, avocado, tomato, layer of ranch dressing, top roll.

BUFFALO CHICKEN DIP SLIDERS

The perfect addition to any game-day appetizer menu, these sliders aim to be everyone's favorite. Serve with your favorite toppings and sides.

2 tablespoons (30 ml) vegetable oil

2 to 3 cups chopped boneless, skinless chicken breast

1½ teaspoons Waltwins Usual Suspects Seasoning (page 52)

1 (8-ounce, or 225 g) brick cream cheese

½ cup (120 ml) Frank's RedHot Buffalo Wings Sauce

½ cup (58 g) shredded cheddar cheese

½ cup (120 g) ranch or blue cheese dressing

1. Bring the griddle to medium-low heat.

2. Pour the oil on the grill and put the chicken on it. Season with the Usual Suspects Seasoning. Cook for 3 to 4 minutes, flip the chicken, and cook for 3 to 4 minutes more, or until the chicken is cooked through, no longer pink, and reaches an internal temperature of 165°F (74°C).

3. Place the cream cheese brick on the chicken and let it melt while stirring it into the chicken. Pour on the hot sauce and add the cheddar, letting it melt while stirring. Finally, top with the ranch dressing. Once all ingredients are mixed, pull the chicken off the griddle and spread it generously on the Hawaiian rolls to serve.

BUFFALO CHICKEN CHEESESTEAK SANDWICHES

SERVES 4

This recipe was the biggest hit at our last Fourth of July party. If you want chicken cheesesteaks that bring just enough heat to wake you up, but not take you down, this recipe is just what you need.

---

3 tablespoons (45 ml) vegetable oil, divided

2 tablespoons (28 g) unsalted butter, divided

1 large yellow onion, diced

1 tablespoon (18 g) salt, divided

2 teaspoons ground black pepper, divided

1 pound (454 g) boneless, skinless chicken breast, cut into 1-inch (2.5 cm) cubes

½ cup (120 ml) Frank's RedHot Buffalo Wings Hot Sauce

12 slices provolone cheese

4 hoagie rolls, split horizontally

½ cup (120 g) ranch or blue cheese dressing

1. Bring the griddle to medium-low heat.

2. Pour 1 tablespoon (15 ml) of oil onto the griddle, followed by the butter. As soon as the butter melts, place the onion in the butter and add 1 teaspoon of salt and 1 teaspoon of pepper. Cook for 5 to 6 minutes, moving the onion slowly until it begins to turn translucent. Push the onion to a cooler side of the griddle, not over direct heat, or set aside off the griddle.

3. Pour the remaining 2 tablespoons (30 ml) of oil onto the griddle and lay the chicken in the oil. Season with the remaining 2 teaspoons of salt and 1 teaspoon of pepper. Cook, slowly stirring the chicken, until it begins to cook through, then stir and chop the chicken with a scraper to break it up into small chunks and pieces. Mix the onion in with the chicken.

4. Pour the wing sauce over the chicken and mix until the sauce is evenly distributed. Divide the buffalo chicken into four even lines (the length of the hoagie rolls) and lay three slices of provolone on each line of chicken.

5. Place the hoagie rolls on the griddle for about 1 minute to heat up the outside of each roll. Open each roll and lay one roll facedown on each line of cheesesteak. Let sit for about 30 seconds, then with a spatula, scoop up the cheesesteak, holding firm to the roll and turn the sandwich right-side up. Spread ranch over the top to serve.

CHICKEN SMASH SLIDERS

If you like chicken, and you like sliders, these will knock your socks off!

1 pound (454 g) ground chicken

4 to 8 teaspoons (16 to 32 g) Waltwins Usual Suspects Seasoning (page 52)

8 slider buns

Mayonnaise for serving

Mustard for serving

Shredded lettuce for serving

Dill pickle chips for serving

1 to 2 tablespoons (15 to 30 ml) vegetable oil

8 slices provolone cheese

1. Bring the griddle to medium-low heat.

2. While the griddle heats, divide the ground chicken into eight equal (2-ounce, or 56.75 g) portions and roll each into a ball. Season each chicken meatball generously with Usual Suspects Seasoning (½ to 1 teaspoon per meatball). Dress the bottom buns with mayonnaise, mustard, lettuce, and pickles. Set aside.

3. Pour 1 to 2 tablespoons (15 to 30 ml) of oil onto the griddle and spread it out with a spatula. Place the chicken meatballs onto the griddle, spreading them out so they don't smash into one another. One at a time, press the meatballs for 10 seconds on each patty. Once all have been pressed, flip the patties, starting with the first one you pressed. Place a slice of provolone on each patty. Place the top bun on each patty. Once all of the patties are covered, start pulling them off the griddle and serve on the dressed bottom buns.

MARGARITA CHICKEN

Sometimes, a simple, healthy option hits the spot perfectly. Our margarita chicken does just that!

---

2 thin chicken breast fillets

1½ cups (360 ml) margarita mix

4 tablespoons (60 ml) freshly squeezed lime juice, divided

Salt and ground black pepper

1 teaspoon garlic powder

1 (5.6-ounce, or 156 g) packet Spanish rice (preferably Knorr)

1 (15-ounce, or 425 g) can black beans, rinsed and drained

1 tablespoon (15 ml) vegetable oil

1. In a gallon (3.8 L)-size resealable plastic bag, combine the chicken, margarita mix, 2 tablespoons (30 ml) of lime juice, 1 teaspoon of salt, 1 teaspoon of pepper, and the garlic powder. Seal the bag and massage the ingredients to combine and coat the chicken, making sure all of the chicken is covered in the mixture. Refrigerate to marinate for 1 to 2 hours.

2. Prepare the Spanish rice according to the package directions. Warm the black beans.

3. Bring the griddle to medium-low heat.

4. Pour the oil onto the griddle and let heat until you see a wisp of white smoke. Remove the chicken from the marinade and place it in the hot oil. Discard the marinade. Cook for 2 to 3 minutes. Turn the chicken and cook for 2 minutes more.

5. Pour the remaining 2 tablespoons (30 ml) of lime juice over the chicken and season lightly with salt and pepper. Continue cooking and flipping the chicken for 1 minute per side until the internal temperature of the chicken reaches 165°F (74°C). Pull the chicken off the griddle and serve with the Spanish rice and black beans on the side.

TERIYAKI CHICKEN SANDWICHES

I remember the first time I made a simple teriyaki sauce—I felt like a champion! It has always been one of our favorite savory and sweet sauces, so making our own was a dream to us. This sandwich was everything we hoped it would be, and yes, it absolutely needs the pineapple.

FOR TERIYAKI MARINADE:

1 cup (240 ml) water

1 cup (240 ml) soy sauce

1 cup (225 g) packed brown sugar

4 garlic cloves, chopped

1 tablespoon (15 ml) Worcestershire sauce

½ teaspoon onion powder

½ teaspoon grated peeled fresh ginger

FOR CHICKEN:

4 boneless, skinless chicken breast fillets

2 teaspoons salt

1½ teaspoons ground black pepper

1 tablespoon (15 ml) vegetable oil

4 slices deli ham

4 slices Swiss cheese

4 kaiser rolls, split horizontally

2 tablespoons (30 g) mayonnaise, plus more as needed

4 large lettuce leaves

1 tomato, cut into slices

4 pineapple slices

1. To make the teriyaki marinade (on the stovetop): Combine all the marinade ingredients in a medium-size saucepan and bring to a boil over high heat. Boil for 3 to 4 minutes, stirring occasionally, until the sugar dissolves. Remove from the heat and let cool.

2. To make the chicken: Season the chicken with salt and pepper and place in a gallon (3.8 L)-size resealable plastic bag. Pour in the cooled teriyaki marinade to completely cover the chicken. Reserve any excess marinade to use as a sauce. Seal the bag and refrigerate the chicken to marinate for at least 2 hours.

3. Bring the griddle to medium-low heat.

4. Pour the oil onto the griddle. Remove the chicken from the marinade and place it in the oil. Discard the used marinade. Cook for 3 minutes, flip the chicken, and cook for 2 minutes more, keeping an eye on it to ensure it does not burn. If it begins to turn dark brown, flip it again and continue cooking until the internal temperature reaches 165°F (74°C). Once on the final side of cooking, lay one ham slice and one cheese slice on each fillet to melt the cheese.

5. While the chicken finishes cooking, spread a small amount of mayonnaise on the cut sides of each roll and lay the rolls on the griddle over low heat, mayo-side down, away from the chicken. Toast the rolls until they begin to brown lightly, then transfer to a plate.

6. Pull the chicken off the griddle and build each sandwich: Bottom roll, lettuce, chicken with ham and cheese, tomato, pineapple. Spread the top bun with more mayo. Before placing the top bun on the sandwich, drizzle 1½ teaspoons of the reserved marinade onto the sandwich. Place the top bun on the sandwich, repeat for the second sandwich, and enjoy!

CHICKEN STREET TACOS WITH CREAMY JALAPEÑO RANCH

Take Taco Tuesday to the next level with these amazing chicken street tacos. This one has our family coming over for more week after week.

FOR CREAMY JALAPEÑO RANCH:

1 (1-ounce, or 28 g) packet ranch dressing mix

1 cup (240 ml) milk

1 cup (240 g) mayonnaise

1 or 2 medium-size jalapeño peppers, seeded and finely chopped

2 tablespoons (2 g) finely chopped fresh cilantro

1 to 2 tablespoons (15 to 30 ml) freshly squeezed lime juice

1 to 2 teaspoons dill pickle brine

FOR CHICKEN STREET TACOS:

2 tablespoons (24 g) Tajín seasoning

1 tablespoon (12 g) Waltwins Usual Suspects Seasoning (page 52)

2 pounds (908 g) boneless, skinless chicken thighs

2 tablespoons (30 ml) vegetable oil

3 limes, halved

8 to 10 (4½-inch, or 11 cm) street-size taco flour tortillas

1 cup (115 g) shredded Mexican-style cheese blend

½ cup (8 g) chopped fresh cilantro

1. To make the creamy jalapeño ranch: In a medium-size bowl, whisk all the dressing ingredients well. Cover and refrigerate for at least 30 minutes before serving.

2. To make the street tacos: In a small bowl, stir together the Tajín seasoning and Usual Suspects Seasoning. Set aside.

3. Pound the chicken thighs out as flat as possible, about ⅛ to ¼ inch (0.3 to 0.6 cm) thick, without breaking or tearing the meat.

4. Bring the griddle to medium-low heat.

5. Pour the oil onto the griddle and place the chicken thighs in the oil. Cook for 2 to 3 minutes, or until the chicken is about halfway cooked (light brown in color). Season the top of the chicken thighs liberally with about half of the Tajín mixture and squeeze two lime halves over the chicken. Flip the chicken thighs and season them with the remaining Tajín mixture. Squeeze two more lime halves over the chicken and cook for 2 minutes, or until the internal temperature reaches at least 165°F (74°C). Pull the chicken off the griddle and let it rest for 5 minutes. Cut the chicken meat into ¼-inch (0.6 cm) strips.

6. Place the tortillas onto a clean area of the warm griddle for about 30 seconds. On each tortilla, place a small handful of shredded cheese, four or five strips of chicken, a drizzle of jalapeño ranch, and cilantro to taste. Serve with the remaining lime halves for squeezing.

CHICKEN STIR-FRY

When you make this chicken stir-fry, no one will believe it wasn't from a Japanese steak house. Blow them all away when you let them watch you create the magic right in front of their drooling eyes.

FOR STIR-FRY SAUCE:

1 cup (240 ml) chicken broth

¼ cup (62.5) hoisin sauce

2 tablespoons (30 ml) soy sauce

2 teaspoons sesame oil

1 tablespoon (8 g) cornstarch

FOR CHICKEN STIR-FRY:

2 to 3 tablespoons (30 to 45 ml)
    vegetable oil, divided

1 red bell pepper, cut into 2-inch
    (5 cm) slices

1 yellow bell pepper, cut into 2-inch
    (5 cm) slices

1 orange bell pepper, cut into 2-inch
    (5 cm) slices

½ yellow onion, cut into 2-inch (5 cm) strips

3 cups (210 g) broccoli florets

1 to 2 tablespoons (14 to 28 g)
    unsalted butter

Salt and ground black pepper

1½ teaspoons garlic paste

1 teaspoon ginger paste

1 pound (454 g) chicken breast,
    cut into ½-inch (1 cm) cubes

Sliced scallion for garnish

Sesame seeds for garnish

1. To make the stir-fry sauce: In a medium-size bowl, whisk all the sauce ingredients until combined. Set aside.

2. Bring the griddle to medium-low heat.

3. To make the chicken stir-fry: Pour 1 tablespoon (15 ml) of vegetable oil onto the griddle and place the bell peppers, onion, and broccoli in it. Add the butter and incorporate it into the vegetables. Season the vegetables with salt and pepper. Cook the vegetables for about 10 minutes, slowly mixing, or until the onion becomes translucent.

4. On another part of the griddle, combine 1 tablespoon (15 ml) of vegetable oil, the garlic paste, and ginger paste and mix to combine and cook until the garlic begins to brown (do not wait too long or the garlic will burn). Place the chicken on the garlic-ginger mixture and cook, stirring, for 4 to 6 minutes, or until the chicken is no longer pink and the internal temperature reaches 165°F (74°C).

5. Mix the cooked chicken with the vegetables. Pour in the stir-fry sauce a little at a time, using as much or as little sauce as you like. Serve garnished with the scallion and sesame seeds.

CHICKEN FRIED RICE

This was the first fried rice we ever tried on the griddle, and the one we have made the most! It's easy to get just right and a "must do" for anyone trying to figure out how to make fried rice. The chicken is the perfect protein with white rice, especially jasmine rice! Look for sweet soy sauce at any Asian market. Note: You do need to cook and cool the rice ahead; overnight is best, so keep that in mind when planning for this dish.

4 cups (800 g) jasmine rice

4 to 5 tablespoons (60 to 75 ml) vegetable oil, divided

2 garlic cloves, minced

8 tablespoons (1 stick, or 112 g) unsalted butter

2 to 3 teaspoons (15 ml) sesame oil

1 (12-ounce, or 340 g) bag mixed frozen veggies (corn, peas, carrots)

½ medium-size yellow onion, diced

4 large eggs

2 pounds (908 g) boneless, skinless chicken breast, cut into 1-inch (2.5 cm) cubes

Sweet soy sauce or regular soy sauce for seasoning

1 to 2 tablespoons (8 to 16 g) sesame seeds

1. Cook the rice according to the package directions. Spread it out on a baking sheet and refrigerate, on the sheet, overnight to cool and dry.

2. Bring the griddle to medium-low heat.

3. Pour 2 tablespoons (30 ml) of vegetable oil onto the griddle and place the garlic and butter in the oil, immediately followed by the rice. Stir-fry the rice for 5 to 7 minutes in the garlic butter. Mix in the sesame oil.

4. On a separate area of the griddle, also over medium-low heat, combine the vegetables and onion.

5. While the vegetables cook, place 1 tablespoon (15 ml) of oil next to the rice and crack the eggs into the oil. Once the eggs begin to cook, lightly scramble them for a minute or two, then mix the eggs into the rice.

6. Once the vegetables are hot and cooked, move them to a section of the griddle that is no longer on to keep warm.

7. Pour another 1 to 2 tablespoons (15 to 30 ml) of oil onto the griddle where the vegetables were and put the chicken it in. Stir-fry the chicken until it is cooked through and no longer pink. While the chicken cooks, season the veggies, chicken, and rice with sweet soy sauce to taste. Once the chicken is cooked through, mix it with the veggies, rice, and eggs. Taste and add more soy sauce until you like the taste. Sprinkle with sesame seeds and enjoy!

SIMPLY AMAZING CHEESY QUESADILLAS

This "how to" recipe may change the way you do quesadillas forever. From the first time Adam's wife made these quesadillas this way, Adam has been hooked, and it's just about the only way we make quesadillas now.

---

4 tablespoons (½ stick, or 56 g) unsalted butter, at room temperature

8 (6-inch, or 15 cm) taco-size flour tortillas

3 cups (345 g) shredded Mexican-style cheese blend

1. Bring the griddle to medium-low heat.

2. While the griddle heats, spread butter on one side of each tortilla. Once the griddle is to temperature, place four tortillas, butter-side down, on the griddle. Spread ¾ cup (86.25 g) of cheese over each tortilla and top each with a second tortilla, butter-side up. Cook for 3 to 5 minutes. Check the bottom of the tortillas and flip the quesadillas when the tortilla begins to turn golden brown. Cook for about 4 minutes more, or until the second side is golden brown and the cheese is melty.

HONEY GARLIC CHICKEN

When we first began making Asian-inspired dishes, we felt that what made them so delicious was all the ingredients and how seemingly "complicated" they were. With this honey garlic chicken, we found that less is more and simple can lead to simply delicious! Serve with your favorite sides; we like jasmine rice with this.

---

2 (8-ounce, or 225 g each) boneless, skinless chicken breasts

Salt and ground black pepper

½ cup (60 g) all-purpose flour

3 tablespoons (45 ml) olive oil, divided

3 tablespoons (42 g) unsalted butter

2 garlic cloves, minced

1½ tablespoons (23 ml) apple cider vinegar

1 tablespoon (15 ml) soy sauce

⅓ cup (107 g) honey

¼ cup (25 g) chopped scallion, white and green parts

1. Bring one area of the griddle to high heat and another area to medium-high heat.

2. Pat the chicken dry with a paper towel and season liberally with salt and pepper. Place the flour in a shallow bowl and season with salt and pepper. Dredge the chicken in the flour, coating both sides evenly.

3. Pour 2 tablespoons (30 ml) of oil onto the area of the griddle that is at medium-high heat. Let heat until you see a wisp of white smoke.

4. At the same time, place a large skillet on the griddle over high heat, pour in the remaining 1 tablespoon (15 ml) of oil, and add the butter to melt. Add the garlic, stirring to prevent burning.

5. Lay the coated chicken in the hot oil over medium-high heat and cook for 3 minutes per side.

6. In the skillet, combine the vinegar, soy sauce, and honey with the garlic, stirring to combine. Cook for 2 to 3 minutes to thicken the sauce slightly. Place the chicken in the skillet and cook for 4 to 5 minutes in the sauce, or until the internal temperature of the chicken reaches at least 165°F (74°C). Serve garnished with scallion.

WALTWINS ORANGE CHICKEN

This cook still stands out as one of our all-time biggest surprises. If you like Panda Express's Orange Chicken, you will love this.

FOR CHICKEN:

2½ pounds (1.1 kg) boneless, skinless chicken thighs, cut into 1-inch (2.5 cm) cubes

1 tablespoon (18 g) salt

1 tablespoon (8 g) cornstarch

1 teaspoon ground white pepper

3 tablespoons (22.5 g) all-purpose flour

1 large egg

3 to 5 tablespoons (45 to 75 ml) vegetable oil

FOR ORANGE SAUCE:

1 tablespoon (15 ml) vegetable oil

¼ teaspoon red pepper flakes

1 tablespoon (10 g) minced garlic

½ teaspoon minced peeled fresh ginger

¼ cup (50 g) granulated sugar

¼ cup (56 g) packed light brown sugar

¼ cup (60 ml) freshly squeezed orange juice

¼ cup (60 ml) distilled white vinegar

2 tablespoons (30 ml) soy sauce

2 tablespoons (16 g) cornstarch

2 tablespoons (30 ml) water

1 teaspoon sesame oil

1. To make the chicken: In a large bowl, combine the chicken, salt, cornstarch, white pepper, flour, and egg. Mix thoroughly to coat.

2. Bring the griddle to medium-low heat.

3. Line a large plate with paper towels.

4. Pour about 3 tablespoons (45 ml) of vegetable oil onto the griddle and let heat until you see a wisp of white smoke. Gently add the chicken to the hot oil and cook for 5 to 6 minutes, turning and adding more oil, if needed, until lightly golden brown. Transfer the chicken to the prepared plate.

5. Bring the griddle to medium-high heat.

6. To make the orange sauce: Place a medium-size pan on the griddle and pour in the vegetable oil. Let heat until it shimmers. Add the red pepper flakes, garlic, and ginger and cook for 30 seconds, stirring constantly, until fragrant. Stir in the granulated sugar and brown sugar. Pour in the orange juice. Cook, stirring occasionally, while the sugars begin to dissolve in the liquid. Pour in the vinegar and soy sauce and stir to combine.

7. In a small bowl, whisk the cornstarch and water until the cornstarch dissolves. Whisk this slurry into the sauce and cook until the sauce is a syrupy consistency.

8. Add the chicken to the sauce and stir until completely coated. Drizzle with the sesame oil, stirring the oil into the chicken and sauce. Serve and enjoy!

CHICKEN KATSU

SERVES 6 TO 8

Adam was a college student in Hawaii, where L&L Hawaiian Barbecue became a favorite local place to eat—and eat chicken katsu. But chicken katsu is so simple to make at home and the sauce is divine. This version will give you a taste of the islands and a plate lunch special!

FOR KATSU SAUCE:

3 cups (720 ml) water, divided

1 cup (240 g) ketchup

1 cup (200 g) sugar

½ cup (120 ml) Worcestershire sauce

⅓ teaspoon salt

¼ teaspoon chicken bouillon

¼ teaspoon ground white pepper

¼ teaspoon garlic powder

2 or 3 dashes hot sauce

½ teaspoon cornstarch

FOR CHICKEN:

4 pounds (1.8 kg) boneless, skinless chicken thighs

2 large eggs

¾ cup (96 g) cornstarch

¼ teaspoon salt

¼ teaspoon ground white pepper

¼ teaspoon garlic powder

1 cup (240 ml) water

1 pound (454 g) panko breadcrumbs

3 tablespoons (45 ml) vegetable oil, plus more as needed

1. To make the katsu sauce: In a saucepan over medium-high heat, stir together 2½ cups (600 ml) of water, the ketchup, sugar, Worcestershire sauce, salt, chicken bouillon, white pepper, garlic powder, and hot sauce. Bring to a boil, stirring occasionally, and cook until the sugar dissolves. In a small bowl, whisk the cornstarch and remaining ½ cup (120 ml) of water until the cornstarch dissolves. Whisk this slurry into the sauce and cook until thickened. Remove from the heat.

2. To make the chicken: Open the chicken thighs and flatten them between two sheets of parchment paper.

3. In a large bowl, whisk the eggs, cornstarch, salt, white pepper, garlic powder, and water to make a batter. Place the breadcrumbs in a shallow bowl. Coat each piece of chicken in the egg batter, then in the breadcrumbs, making sure to coat the entire surface of the chicken.

4. Bring the griddle to medium-low heat.

5. Pour the oil onto the griddle and let heat until you see a wisp of white smoke. Place the coated chicken in the hot oil and cook for about 2 minutes, or until the bottom is golden brown. Carefully flip the chicken in the hot oil, adding more if needed, and cook for 2 minutes, or until golden brown and the internal temperature reaches 165°F (74°C).

6. Dunk the chicken in the sauce to serve, passing extra sauce at the table.

HAWAIIAN BARBECUE CHICKEN

SERVES 8

Going back to his time as a college student in Hawaii, almost more than ordering Chicken Katsu (page 77), Adam would grab a Hawaiian barbecue chicken plate lunch whenever he could! This easy recipe is a fast adaptation for that island flare when you don't have access to all the island-favorite ingredients! Serve with Hawaiian Macaroni Salad (page 45) for the complete experience.

---

3 cups (720 ml) soy sauce

1 cup (200 g) sugar

1 cup (240 ml) water

½ teaspoon minced peeled fresh ginger

¼ teaspoon minced garlic

¼ teaspoon ground black pepper

4 pounds (1.8 kg) boneless, skinless chicken thighs

2 to 3 tablespoons (30 to 45 ml) vegetable oil

1. In a large bowl, whisk the soy sauce, sugar, water, ginger, garlic, and pepper to blend. Add the chicken, turning it to coat in the marinade. Cover and refrigerate for at least 5 hours.

2. When ready to cook, bring the griddle to medium-low heat.

3. Pour the oil onto the griddle and let heat until you see a wisp of white smoke. Remove the chicken from the marinade and lay it in the hot oil. Discard the marinade. Cook for 3 to 4 minutes, checking to ensure the chicken is not burning. (It will darken, and some spots may look burned, but it is the caramelization of the marinade.) Flip the chicken to cook the other side for 3 minutes. Flip the chicken a final time and cook until the internal temperature is at least 165°F (74°C). Pull the chicken from the grill and serve.

BREADED CHICKEN PARMESAN

SERVES 2

A favorite of Brett's, breaded chicken Parmesan was one of his first requests to make on the griddle, and are we ever happy we finally did this version.

1 (24-ounce, or 675 g) jar Cabernet marinara sauce or plain marinara

1½ cups (360 ml) buttermilk

2 teaspoons salt

2 teaspoons ground black pepper

2 cups (220 g) Italian-style seasoned breadcrumbs

1 large chicken breasts fillet, cut into two thin cutlets

3 to 5 tablespoons (45 to 75 ml) vegetable oil

4 slices mozzarella cheese

Cooked angel hair pasta for serving

1. Bring one burner of the griddle to medium heat.

2. Pour the marinara into a medium-size saucepan and place the pan on the griddle. Cook for 10 minutes until warmed through.

3. While the sauce warms, bring another area of the griddle to medium heat.

4. As the grill heats, pour the buttermilk into a shallow bowl and whisk in the salt and pepper. Put the breadcrumbs in another shallow bowl. Place one chicken breast cutlet in the buttermilk and ensure it is completely covered. Pull the chicken from the buttermilk and place it in the breadcrumbs, ensuring the entire breast is completely covered with breadcrumbs. Repeat with remaining cutlet.

5. Pour 2 to 3 tablespoons (30 to 45 ml) of oil into the middle of the second cooking area and let heat until you see a wisp of white smoke. Place the chicken in the hot oil and cook for 2 minutes. Flip the chicken and cook for 1 to 2 minutes.

6. Spoon a thin layer of marinara onto each chicken cutlet and place 2 mozzarella slices on each. Cook until the cheese melts and the internal temperature of the chicken reaches 165°F (74°C). Serve the chicken over the angel hair and pass the remaining marinara to pour over the chicken and pasta.

KOREAN-STYLE FLAVOR BOMB HONEY WINGS

SERVES 6

Korean-style dishes are packed with flavor. Here, we combine our use of the griddle for cooking the wings with an amazingly flavored umami bomb Korean-style honey wing sauce to create a dish with some kick. You will not be disappointed.

FOR SAUCE:

¼ cup (60 ml) soy sauce

¼ cup (60 g) gochujang

2 tablespoons (30 ml) rice vinegar

2 tablespoons (40 g) honey

2 tablespoons (20 g) minced garlic

1 tablespoon (15 ml) sesame oil

1 tablespoon (6 g) minced peeled
    fresh ginger

FOR WINGS:

3 pounds (1.3 kg) chicken wings

1 tablespoon (18 g) salt

4 teaspoons (8 g) ground black pepper

2 teaspoons garlic powder

3 tablespoons (45 ml) vegetable oil

1. To make the sauce: In a large bowl, whisk the soy sauce, gochujang, vinegar, honey, garlic, sesame oil, and ginger until blended. Set aside.

2. To make the wings: In another large bowl, combine the wings, salt, pepper, and garlic powder. Mix to ensure an even coating.

3. Bring the griddle to medium heat.

4. Spread the vegetable oil across the surface of the griddle and place the wings in the oil, spreading them out evenly. Cook for 4 to 5 minutes, covering the wings with a dome or griddle hood, until they begin to turn golden brown on the bottom. Flip the wings and cook for 4 to 5 minutes, covered, on the second side until golden. Flip the wings again and cook, covered, for 3 to 4 minutes, watching to ensure the wings do not burn. Flip and repeat. Continue cooking and flipping until the internal temperature of the wings is at least 165°F (74 C), although we recommend 180°F (82°C) for crispier wings. Total cook time can be between 20 and 30 minutes; larger wings can take up to 45 minutes.

5. Transfer the fully cooked wings to the bowl with the sauce and toss to coat.

CHICKEN CORDON BLEU

We have come to LOVE the cooks that just seem like they can't be done on the griddle. "Wrong tool, wrong job?" Right?! We say, CHALLENGE ACCEPTED. We collaborated on this recipe to create a stellar griddle-fried chicken cordon bleu.

2 boneless skinless, chicken breasts

3 to 4 teaspoons (12 to 16 g) Waltwins Usual Suspects Seasoning (page 52), plus more for the dredge

2 tablespoons (30 g) honey mustard

8 slices Swiss cheese

2 slices deli ham

1 to 2 cups (120 to 240 g) all-purpose flour

1 cup (240 ml) buttermilk

½ cup (25 g) panko breadcrumbs

1. Bring the griddle to medium heat.

2. While the griddle heats, butterfly the chicken by cutting through the middle of each breast horizontally, but do not cut all the way through the other side. Open the breasts like a book. Pound the chicken breasts to ¼-inch (0.6 cm) thickness. Season each piece of chicken on both sides with the Usual Suspects Seasoning.

3. Spread the honey mustard liberally, to taste, over the inside (the rough side) of the chicken. Place two cheese slices and one ham slice on one side of each breast, then top that with two more cheese slices. Fold each breast over to enclose the ham and cheese.

4. Place the flour in a shallow bowl and season it to taste with the Usual Suspects Seasoning. Whisk with a fork to blend. Pour the buttermilk into another shallow bowl and put the breadcrumbs in a third bowl. Dredge each breast in the flour, ensuring the entire surface (both sides) is completely coated and, being careful to keep the bundle together, submerge both sides in the buttermilk and place the chicken into the breadcrumbs, ensuring complete coverage.

5. Put the chicken on the griddle and cook for 5 minutes, then carefully flip. Continue to cook and flip the chicken until it is no longer pink and the internal temperature reaches 165°F (74°C).

BOURBON CHICKEN

Does bourbon chicken really need bourbon to be considered bourbon chicken? We prove with this recipe that it does not! In fact, this dish carries a common misconception due to its name, which was derived from where it was created: Bourbon Street in New Orleans. With or without bourbon, this dish delivers amazing flavor in every bite. Serve with your favorite side dish.

⅓ cup (75 g) packed brown sugar

⅓ cup (80 ml) soy sauce

¼ cup (60 ml) apple juice

2 tablespoons (30 ml) olive oil

2 tablespoons (30 g) ketchup

1 tablespoon (15 ml) apple cider vinegar

1 garlic clove, minced

¼ teaspoon ground ginger

¾ teaspoon red pepper flakes

2 pounds (908 g) boneless, skinless chicken breast, cut into ½-inch (1 cm) pieces

½ cup (120 ml) water plus 2 tablespoons (30 ml)

1 tablespoon (8 g) cornstarch

1. Bring one side of the griddle to high heat and the other side to medium-low heat.

2. In a medium-size skillet over high heat, stir together the brown sugar, soy sauce, apple juice, oil, ketchup, vinegar, garlic, ginger, and red pepper flakes. Bring to a boil. (On the griddle, this will take longer than on the stovetop; to speed up the process, cook the sauce on the stovetop.)

3. While the sauce heats, place the chicken on the griddle over medium-low heat. Cook, turning occasionally, until the chicken is light brown and nearly cooked through.

4. Once the sauce comes to a rolling boil, in a small bowl, whisk the water and cornstarch until the cornstarch dissolves. Whisk this slurry into the sauce. Return the sauce to a boil, reduce the heat to medium, and cook until it reaches your desired thickness.

5. Pour the sauce over the chicken on the griddle, cooking, mixing, and stirring, until the chicken is thoroughly cooked and no longer pink and the sauce coats the chicken nicely.

BODACIOUS BURGERS

INSIDE-OUT DOUBLE-DOUBLE BURGERS WITH FAMOUS COPYCAT SAUCE

SERVES 2

If you know, YOU KNOW! In-N-Out is a coveted favorite of Californians. We grew up craving their burgers, which we had never had, so when we finally had the chance to eat one, we understood the hype. Our Inside-Out copycat sauce takes the smash burger favorite to the next level.

FOR COPYCAT SAUCE:

⅓ cup (75 g) mayonnaise

2 tablespoons (30 g) sweet relish

2 tablespoons (30 g) ketchup

1 teaspoon sugar

1 teaspoon distilled white vinegar

¼ teaspoon salt, plus more as needed

¼ teaspoon ground black pepper, plus more as needed

Dash of Worcestershire sauce

FOR DOUBLE-DOUBLE BURGERS:

8 ounces (225 g) 80/20 ground beef

1 tablespoon (14 g) unsalted butter

1 medium-size yellow onion, diced

2 hamburger buns (preferably potato buns)

2 to 3 tablespoons (30 to 45 ml) vegetable oil

Salt and ground black pepper

Yellow mustard for seasoning

2 slices American cheese

2 slices beefsteak tomato

2 iceberg lettuce leaves

1. To make the copycat sauce: In a small bowl, stir together all the sauce ingredients until well blended. Taste and season with more salt and pepper, if needed. Cover and refrigerate for at least 1 hour before serving.

2. To make the double-double burgers: Divide the ground beef into four equal portions and roll each into a ball, then flatten each into a 4-inch (10 cm) patty and set aside.

3. Bring the griddle to medium-low heat.

4. Place the butter on the griddle to melt. Add the onion to the butter and sauté until the onion begins to brown and become translucent. Pull the onion from the heat.

5. Bring another area of the griddle to medium heat.

6. One minute before placing the patties on the griddle, toast the buns, cut-side down first, then flip and toast the outside for a moment as well.

7. Pour 1 to 2 tablespoons (15 to 30 ml) of oil onto the griddle and place the patties in the oil. Season each patty with salt and pepper. Cook for 1 minute. Top each patty with about 3 swirls of mustard, then flip each patty and cook in the mustard for 1 minute. While the second side cooks, place 1 slice of American cheese on two of the patties to melt.

8. To build the burgers: Place the bottom buns, cut-side up, on plates. Spread 1 tablespoon (15 ml) of sauce on each bottom bun. Top each bottom bun with one tomato slice, one lettuce leaf, and a second tablespoon (15 ml) of sauce. Add the cheese-topped patty, a heap of sautéed onions, the second patty, and then the top bun.

ROCKY MOUNTAIN SMASH BURGERS

SERVES 2

Growing up in Utah, there was a favorite place our dad would frequent: Rocky Mountain Drive-In, which sadly closed its doors. This burger was a legend to us! Brett first made this version, and since then, it has become one of our absolute favorite smash burger recipes.

2 potato hamburger buns, split

12 ounces (340 g) 80/20 ground beef

1 to 2 tablespoons (15 to 30 ml) vegetable oil

1 teaspoon salt

1 teaspoon ground black pepper

4 thin slices deli ham

4 slices American cheese

Fry Sauce (recipe follows) for serving

Pickle chips for serving

Shredded lettuce for serving

½ yellow onion, cut into ¼-inch (0.6 cm)-thick rounds

1. Bring the griddle to high heat.

2. While the griddle is coming to temperature, toast both sides of each bun on the griddle until lightly browned. Set the buns aside.

3. Divide the ground beef into four equal (3-ounce, or 85 g) portions and roll each into a loosely packed ball.

4. Pour the oil onto the griddle and place the meatballs in the oil, spread out so they don't smash into one another. Cook for 30 seconds, then smash each meatball all the way down flat with a burger smasher or the back side of a spatula, using the backside of another spatula to help apply pressure, holding the smash for 10 to 15 seconds. Season the burgers with salt and pepper. Cook until you see the juices begin to rise to the surface (nearly immediately), then quickly flip the burgers with a spatula.

5. Place two slices of ham and one slice of cheese on two of the burgers. Place one slice of cheese on each of the other two burgers. Pull each burger from the heat; the cheese will continue to melt while building the burger.

6. Place the burger with one slice of cheese only on the bottom buns and top with the ham-and-cheese–topped burgers. Top with fry sauce, pickles, shredded lettuce, onion, and the top bun to finish.

(see next page for Fry Sauce)

FRY SAUCE

MAKES 2 CUPS (480 G)

Growing up in Utah, fry sauce is a simple yet necessary sauce for fries, burgers, chicken tenders, and so much more.

1 cup (240 g) mayonnaise, plus more as needed

1 cup (240 g) ketchup, plus more as needed

1 to 2 teaspoons pickle brine

½ teaspoon celery salt

In a medium-size bowl, whisk the mayo, ketchup, pickle brine, and celery salt until combined and the sauce is a nice pink hue. Taste and add more mayo or ketchup (we like 2 tablespoons, or 30 g, more ketchup). Cover and refrigerate for at least 30 minutes before serving.

FAMOUS BEEF 'N' CHEDDAR COPYCAT WITH SASSY SAUCE

As far as copycat recipes go, this one caught us by surprise. It had been highly requested, and so we wanted to give it a shot—and we think we nailed it.

FOR SASSY SAUCE:

1 cup (240 g) ketchup

2 teaspoons water, plus more as needed

1 teaspoon garlic powder, plus more as needed

FOR FAMOUS BEEF 'N' CHEDDAR COPYCAT:

2 tablespoons (28 g) unsalted butter

2 tablespoons (15 g) all-purpose flour

2 cups (480 ml) whole milk

2 cups (230 g) shredded cheddar cheese

Shredded American cheese for the sauce

1 to 2 teaspoons salt

1 pound (454 g) thinly sliced deli roast beef

4 onion buns

1. To make the sassy sauce: In a small bowl, stir together the ketchup, water, and garlic powder until blended. Taste and adjust as needed (we add a bit more garlic powder and water to thin the sauce, similar to the original).

2. To make the cheddar sauce: In a medium-size saucepan, on the stovetop or griddle over medium-high heat, melt the butter. Stir in the flour to create a roux (a cooked mixture of flour and fat used as a thickener in a soup or a sauce). As soon as the flour is incorporated into the butter, stirring constantly, pour in the milk a little at a time. As the roux thickens, add more milk, stirring, until all the milk is incorporated. Add the cheddar and mix until the cheese is completely melted. Stir in the American cheese to taste and salt (begin with 1 teaspoon) until you like how the sauce tastes. Keep warm (the cheese sauce will begin to solidify when cooling; to reuse, gently reheat the cheese sauce).

3. Bring a separate area of the griddle to medium-low heat. Place the roast beef slices on the griddle and cook for about 1 minute per side, just long enough to get the meat hot. Pull the meat from the heat. Place the buns, cut-side down, on the griddle for about 1 minute, or until the inside is lightly toasted.

4. To build the sandwich: Spread a spoonful of sassy sauce on the bottom bun. Stack the roast beef about an inch (2.5 cm) thick on the bottom bun and add a generous drizzle of cheese sauce. Spread another spoonful of sauce on the inside of the top bun and place the bun on the sandwich.

OKLAHOMA ONION DOUBLE SMASH BURGERS

SERVES 2

As crazy as it sounds, we both grew up not liking onions—like, at all! As we grew our culinary prowess, we began to discover the amazing flavor that onion brings to just about every dish. Then, we discovered the Oklahoma onion smash burger. Simply put, you smash a burger with a bunch of onions in it. The result? Near perfection. Your favorite toppings will make it perfect.

---

10 ounces (280 g) 80/20 ground beef

1 to 2 tablespoons (15 to 30 ml) vegetable oil

½ yellow onion, thinly sliced

½ teaspoon salt

½ teaspoon ground black pepper

4 slices American Cheese

2 hamburger buns

1. Divide the beef into four equal portions and loosely pack each into a ball.

2. Bring the griddle to high heat.

3. Pour the oil onto the griddle, then place the ground beef balls in the oil, spread out so they don't smash into one another.

4. Place a small handful of onion on each meatball. Cook for 30 seconds. Using a burger smasher and the backside of another spatula to help apply pressure, smash each meatball all the way down flat. Hold the smash for 10 to 15 seconds. Once each burger is smashed and you see the juices begin to rise to the surface (nearly immediately), use the spatula to quickly flip them and place one slice of cheese on each burger. Pull the burgers off the griddle (the cheese will continue to melt while building the burger). Place two smash burgers on each bottom bun and top as desired.

JAPANESE "GREETINGS" BURGERS

SERVES 4

This break from the traditional burger will have you breaking tradition more often. This Waltwins version of Red Robin's Banzai Burger is a great cook for the entire family or for a large gathering. You're sure to make everyone feel welcome with this masterpiece.

FOR TERIYAKI SAUCE:

1¾ cups (420 ml) water

1 cup (240 ml) soy sauce

1 cup (225 g) packed brown sugar

½ teaspoon onion powder

½ teaspoon garlic powder

FOR BURGERS:

1 pound (454 g) 80/20 ground beef

1 whole pineapple, trimmed, peeled, cored, and cut into slices, or 1 (20-ounce, or 560 g) can sliced, drained (about 2 slices per burger; save the juice for another use)

1 to 2 tablespoons (15 to 30 ml) vegetable oil

4 slices Swiss or cheddar cheese

4 hamburger buns

1 to 2 tomatoes, sliced

1 head lettuce, shredded

Mayonnaise for serving

1. To make the teriyaki sauce: In a small saucepan over medium heat, whisk all the sauce ingredients to blend. Bring to a boil, then reduce the heat to maintain a simmer and cook for 10 minutes. Remove from the heat and let cool.

2. To make the burgers: Divide the ground beef into four equal (4-ounce, or 113.5 g) portions and form each into a patty. Place each patty into its own sandwich-size resealable plastic bag and divide the teriyaki sauce among the bags. Add two or three pineapple slices to each bag, seal the bags, and refrigerate to marinate for at least 2 hours.

3. Bring the griddle to medium-low heat.

4. Pour the oil onto the griddle. Remove the burgers from the marinade and place them in the oil. Cook for 5 minutes. Flip the burgers, top each with one slice of cheese, and cook for 3 minutes more, then remove from the heat. Once you flip the burgers, remove the pineapple from the marinade and place the slices on the griddle surface and flip once you remove the hamburgers. Cook for 3 minutes more, but watch carefully so it does not burn. If you want to toast the buns, this is the time to do it.

5. Once the burgers, pineapple, and buns are ready, build your burgers on the buns as you like, with pineapple, tomato, lettuce, and mayo to start!

SURF 'N' TURF SMASH BURGERS

How do you make a smash burger even better? You make it a surf 'n' turf.

1 pound (454 g) 80/20 ground beef

1 to 2 teaspoons salt

1 to 2 teaspoons ground black pepper

1 (15-ounce, or 425 g) jar Alfredo sauce

2 tablespoons (30 ml) vegetable oil, divided

1 tablespoon (14 g) unsalted butter

2 garlic cloves, minced

8 ounces (225 g) medium-size raw shrimp, peeled and deveined

1 cup (80 g) shredded Parmesan cheese

½ small red onion, thinly sliced into rings

2 brioche buns

1. Divide the ground beef into four (4-ounce, or 115 g) portions and roll each into a ball. Season with salt and pepper.

2. Bring the griddle to medium-high heat.

3. Pour the Alfredo sauce into a small pot and place on the griddle to warm.

4. Pour 1 tablespoon (15 ml) of oil onto the middle of the griddle and let it heat until you see a wisp of white smoke. Place the butter and garlic in the oil and cook for about 20 seconds—as soon as the garlic begins to turn light brown, it is ready.

5. Put the shrimp in the garlic butter and cook for 2 to 4 minutes until pink and opaque. Remove the shrimp from the griddle.

6. Pour the remaining 1 tablespoon (15 ml) of oil onto the griddle and place the meatballs in it, spreading them out so they don't smash into one another. Cook for 15 to 30 seconds, then start pressing down the burgers, one at a time, holding the press for 10 to 15 seconds to create a sear. Flip the burgers, starting with the first one you pressed.

7. Place a small handful of cheese on each patty, then stack the burgers, making two double stacks.

8. Place onion on the bottom buns, then top the onion with a patty stack on each. Place four to six shrimp on the patties. Pour the Alfredo sauce on top of the patties and add more Parmesan.

9. Place the top bun on and enjoy!

SAN FRANCISCO BURGERS

Can you think of a burger you've had that just teases your mind from time to time creating an insatiable craving? Welcome to our San Francisco Burgers—the tantalizing favorite that is sure to create a permanent craving for this perfectly savory burger. You had me at sourdough!

¼ cup (60 g) ketchup

¼ cup (60 g) mayonnaise

1 tablespoon (15 g) dill pickle relish

1 pound (454 g) 80/20 ground beef

2 to 3 teaspoons (15 ml) Worcestershire sauce

2 to 3 teaspoons (18 g) salt

2 teaspoons ground black pepper

2 to 3 teaspoons (9 g) garlic powder

2 thick-cut bacon slices, halved widthwise

4 slices Swiss cheese

Butter, at room temperature, for cooking

4 slices thick-cut sourdough bread

1 tomato, cut into 4 slices

1. In a small bowl, stir together the ketchup, mayonnaise, and relish until evenly mixed. Set aside (refrigerate if it will be sitting for longer than 1 hour).

2. Bring the griddle to medium-low heat.

3. In a medium-size bowl, combine the ground beef, Worcestershire sauce to taste, salt to taste, pepper, and garlic powder to taste. Mix gently but thoroughly. Divide the mixture in half and form each portion into a large meatball, then form oval patties that will fit on the sourdough bread slices.

4. Cook the bacon on the griddle, flipping, until it is cooked to your desired crispiness. Move the bacon to a cooler side of the griddle, not over direct heat.

5. Place the patties where the bacon was cooked, using the bacon grease. Cook for 4 minutes. Flip the burgers and cook for 1 minute. Place two slices of cheese on each burger and cook for 3 to 4 minutes more, or until the cheese melts and the burger is cooked to your desired doneness.

6. Spread butter on both sides of the bread slices and place them on the griddle. Toast each side to your desired toast-y-ness.

7. To build the burger: Spread the ketchup-mayo sauce on the bottom bread, followed by two tomato slices, the burger, two bacon slices, and the top bread.

FOR BEEF
LOVERS

PASTRAMI PATTY MELTS

It's not often that we give something a try and find that a small "addition" makes such a profound impact, much like adding pastrami to our Patty Melt (page 104)! And although we can eat a patty melt all day, every day, this cook with the addition of pastrami? Next. Level. BOOM!

---

11 ounces (308 g) 80/20 ground beef

5 dashes Worcestershire sauce

Salt and ground black pepper

2 tablespoons (28 g) unsalted butter, plus more for toasting the bread

½ medium-size yellow onion, cut into slices

2 tablespoons (30 ml) vegetable oil

4 ounces (115 g) shaved pastrami

4 slices Swiss cheese

4 slices rye bread

1. In a medium-size bowl, combine the ground beef, Worcestershire sauce, and salt and pepper to taste. Mix, ensuring the ingredients are combined well. Divide the ground beef into two equal portions and form each into a ball.

2. Bring the griddle to medium heat.

3. Use 1 tablespoon (14 g) of butter to coat a small area of the griddle and place the onion on it. Cook the onion until it begins to caramelize, then add the remaining 1 tablespoon (14 g) of butter to the onion. Cook until the onion becomes translucent, then move the onion to a cooler area of the griddle, not over direct heat.

4. Adjust the griddle heat to medium-high heat.

5. Use 2 tablespoons (30 ml) of oil to coat the middle of the griddle. Put the meatballs in the oil, ensuring enough space between them that they don't smash together. Using a burger press, firmly press one burger down onto the griddle, holding the press for 10 seconds. Repeat with other burger. Cook for about 1 minute to create a sear, then flip the burgers.

6. Place the pastrami on the griddle to heat up, moving it constantly until it is hot. Divide the pastrami between the burgers, then top the pastrami with Swiss cheese and let the cheese melt.

7. To toast the bread, coat one side of each rye slice with butter. Place two pieces of bread, butter-side down, on the griddle. Place the burger patties on the bread, then top with onion and the other slice of bread, butter-side up (we put mayonnaise on both sides of the top piece of bread to toast it and add extra flavor to the patty melt). Cook until the bottom bread is toasted, carefully flip the entire sandwich, and toast the top side. Pull the sandwiches off the griddle and let cool slightly before serving.

PATTY MELTS

Many times, we get requests to "try" a new cook we didn't know we needed in our lives. Welcome, Patty Melt. Who knew you were the perfection we were missing?

1 pound (454 g) 80/20 ground beef

2 teaspoons Worcestershire sauce

Salt and ground black pepper

2 to 3 tablespoons (28 to 42 g) unsalted butter, divided

1 medium-size white onion, sliced

1 to 2 tablespoons (15 to 30 ml) vegetable oil

4 slices Swiss cheese

Mayonnaise for serving

8 slices marbled rye bread

1. Bring the griddle to medium-low heat.

2. While the griddle heats, divide the ground beef into four (4-ounce, or 115 g) portions. Mix ½ teaspoon of Worcestershire sauce into each portion and form each into a ball. Season the balls with salt and pepper. Set aside.

3. Place half the butter on the griddle to melt, spreading it out, then place the onion in it. Season with ½ teaspoon of salt and ½ teaspoon of pepper. Cook the onion until it is dark brown, caramelized, and translucent, then pull it off the griddle.

4. Place the remaining butter on the griddle to melt, spreading it out. Place the bread in the butter, toast both sides, then remove it from the griddle.

5. Pour the oil onto the griddle, spread it out with a spatula, and let heat until you see a wisp of white smoke. Place the meatballs in the hot oil, spreading them so they don't smash into one another. Cook for 15 to 30 seconds, then start pressing the burgers, one at a time, holding the press for 10 to 15 seconds to create a sear. Flip the burgers, starting with the first one you pressed, and place one slice of Swiss cheese on each patty to melt. Once the cheese melts, pull the patties from the griddle and turn off the griddle.

6. Spread mayonnaise on one side of each slice of the bread. Place the patties on the mayo and top with caramelized onion. Place the top slice of bread on, mayo-side down, and enjoy!

THE BEST HOMEMADE SLOPPY JOES

"I know you kids like them sloppy!" Just one bite of these sloppy joes will send you straight back to your childhood! Mom may have never made them this good!

⅔ cup (160 g) ketchup

⅓ cup (80 ml) water

1½ tablespoons (23 g) brown sugar

1 tablespoon (16 g) tomato paste

2 teaspoons yellow mustard

1¼ teaspoons Worcestershire sauce

1½ teaspoons Waltwins Usual Suspects Seasoning (page 52)

Salt and ground black pepper

1 teaspoon vegetable oil

1 pound (454 g) 80/20 ground beef

½ large yellow onion, minced

½ green bell pepper, minced

3 garlic cloves, minced

4 to 6 hamburger buns

1. In a medium-size bowl, whisk the ketchup, water, brown sugar, tomato paste, mustard, Worcestershire sauce, Usual Suspects Seasoning, and salt and pepper to taste until smooth and well combined.

2. Bring the griddle to medium heat.

3. Pour the oil onto the griddle and place the ground beef in it. Cook for 5 to 7 minutes, stirring and breaking up the meat into small pieces (the consistency of taco ground beef). Pull the ground beef to the cooler side of the griddle, not over direct heat.

4. Place the onion and bell pepper on the griddle over the heat and sauté for about 3 minutes until soft and the onion is somewhat translucent. Add the garlic and cook for about 30 seconds until fragrant.

5. Mix the ground beef with the bell pepper and onion and pour on the sloppy joe sauce. Mix well. Cook for 5 to 7 minutes more, mixing and moving, until the mixture is cooked to your preferred thickness.

6. Toast the buns, if desired, and serve the sloppy joes on the buns.

CRUNCH-Y WRAP COPYCAT

The Crunchwrap Supreme is one of our Taco Bell favorites, but we don't need to make a run for the border when we have the craving anymore—we make them ourselves.

1 to 2 tablespoons (15 to 30 ml) vegetable oil

1 pound (454 g) 80/20 ground beef

2 tablespoons (18 g) taco seasoning

6 (10-inch, or 25 cm) burrito-size flour tortillas

1 (15-ounce, or 425 g) jar cheese sauce/queso dip

6 tostados

1 (8-ounce, or 225 g) container sour cream

1 (8-ounce, or 225 g) bag shredded iceberg lettuce

1 medium-size tomato, diced

2 cups (230 g) shredded cheddar cheese

6 (6-inch, or 15 cm) taco-size flour tortillas

1. Bring the griddle to medium-low heat.

2. Pour the oil onto the griddle, spread it around with a spatula, and heat until you see a wisp of white smoke. Put the ground beef onto the griddle and cook until browned, chopping it as you go. Stir in the taco seasoning, cook until completely browned, and remove the beef from the griddle. Wipe the griddle clean.

3. Place a 10-inch (25 cm) tortilla on a clean work surface and spread cheese sauce in the middle, creating a circle the size of a tostada. With a small spoon, scoop ground beef onto the cheese circle, covering it. Place a tostada on the beef. Cover the tostada with sour cream, then lettuce, tomato, and cheddar. (Be careful not to make it too thick because the large tortilla needs to fold over most of the ingredients.) Place a 6-inch (15 cm) flour tortilla over the ingredients, then fold the large tortilla up and over the smaller tortilla until it is in the shape of a hexagon. Set aside, folded-side down to prevent the food from spilling out.

4. Repeat step 3 with the remaining ingredients.

5. Place a wrap on the griddle and cook for 15 to 30 seconds, or until the bottom is light brown. Carefully flip the wrap and repeat on the other side. Once both sides are light brown, remove from the griddle. Repeat for each wrap.

MARINATED FLANK STEAK SANDWICHES

Our sister, Angie, is one of the best cooks we know. Several years ago, when living in New York City, she learned this amazing recipe. When we were all back in Utah, where we grew up, Angie prepared these sandwiches for us, which she makes using a grill. Needless to say, this is what we request every time we visit. We have since adapted the cook for the griddle.

½ cup (120 ml) soy sauce

2 tablespoons (30 ml) freshly squeezed
  lemon juice

2 tablespoons (30 ml) vegetable oil

1 tablespoon (3.5 g) dried minced onion

1 large garlic clove, minced

1 teaspoon minced peeled fresh ginger

¼ teaspoon ground black pepper

1 pound (454 g) flank steak

Baguette for serving

Garlic butter, at room temperature,
  for serving

1. In a small bowl, whisk the soy sauce, lemon juice, oil, minced onion, garlic, ginger, and pepper to combine. Place the steak in a gallon (3.8L)-size resealable plastic bag and pour in the marinade. Seal the bag and turn the steak to coat. Refrigerate for 24 to 48 hours (we have found 24 to 36 hours is best), but no longer than 48 hours.

2. Bring one section of the griddle to high heat and another to low heat.

3. Remove the steak from the marinade and place it over high heat. Discard the marinade. Sear the steak for 2 minutes per side. Move the steak to low heat and continue cooking for 4 minutes per side, or until your desired doneness. Pull the steak, wrap it in aluminum foil, and let rest for 20 minutes.

4. Cut open the baguette and spread the insides with the garlic butter.

5. Remove the steak from the foil and cut the steak against the grain into ¼- to ½-inch (0.6 to 1 cm) slices. Fill the baguette with steak slices and cut the baguette sandwich into four pieces to serve.

TRIBUTE TO PHILADELPHIA: TRADITIONAL PHILLY CHEESESTEAKS

SERVES 4

Are we bold enough to call this an "authentic Philly" cheesesteak? We've done our homework, made so many, but rather than alienate an entire city, we will simply pay tribute to, arguably, one of the greatest sandwiches America has produced.

3 tablespoons (45 ml) vegetable oil, divided

3 tablespoons (42 g) unsalted butter

1 large yellow onion, diced

Salt and ground black pepper

1 pound (454 g) rib eye, shaved or sliced as thinly as possible

12 slices provolone cheese

4 hoagie rolls, split horizontally

1. Bring the griddle to medium-low heat.

2. Pour 1 tablespoon (15 ml) of oil onto the griddle, then add the butter to melt. Lay the onion in the melted butter and season with 1 teaspoon of salt and 1 teaspoon of pepper. Cook for 5 to 6 minutes, moving the onion slowly, until it begins to turn translucent. Move the onion to a cooler side of the griddle, not over direct heat, or take it off the griddle.

3. Pour the remaining 2 tablespoons (30 ml) of oil onto the griddle and lay the rib eye in the oil, spreading it out. Season with salt and pepper to taste. Cook the rib eye, spread out and flat, on the griddle for 1 to 2 minutes to create a sear. Once the meat begins to turn brown, indicating it is cooking through, stir and "chop" the rib eye with a scraper to break up the meat. Mix in the onion, then divide the meat and onion into four even lines, each the length of a hoagie roll. Lay three slices of cheese on each line of meat to melt.

4. Place the hoagie rolls on the griddle for about 1 minute to warm the outside of each roll. Open each roll and place one facedown on each line of cheesesteak and let sit for about 30 seconds. Using a spatula, scoop up the cheesesteak, holding firm to the hoagie, and turn the whole sandwich right-side up.

KOREAN-STYLE BARBECUE BEEF (BULGOGI)

This salty, sweet, spicy from the ginger, restaurant-level cook, made at home on your griddle, is a crowd-pleaser. Add your favorite Korean sides, like kimchi, spicy cucumber salad, pickled onions, or pancakes, to complete the meal.

Jasmine rice for serving

⅓ cup (80 ml) soy sauce

2½ tablespoons (38 g) brown sugar

2 tablespoons (30 ml) sesame oil

1 tablespoon (8 g) grated peeled
   fresh ginger

3 garlic cloves, minced

1 bunch scallions, white and green parts,
   chopped, separated

1½ pounds (681 g) New York strip steak
   or sirloin

1½ teaspoons vegetable oil

1. Prepare as much rice as you need for serving according to the package instructions. Keep warm until needed.

2. In a medium-size bowl, whisk the soy sauce, brown sugar, sesame oil, ginger, garlic, and scallion whites to combine. Set aside.

3. Cut the steak into very thin strips and place them in a large resealable plastic bag. Pour in the soy marinade, seal the bag, and turn the steak to coat, ensuring it's covered in the marinade. Refrigerate for at least 1 hour.

4. Bring the griddle to medium-low heat.

5. Pour the vegetable oil onto the griddle. Remove the beef from the marinade and place it in the oil. Discard the marinade. Cook for 1 minute to sear the steak. Flip the steak and cook for 1 minute more. Pull the beef off the griddle and serve over the jasmine rice, garnished with the scallion greens.

MONGOLIAN-STYLE BEEF

Do you have a favorite restaurant dish that stands out in your mind and sends you back to that restaurant time and time again? Mongolian beef has that effect on us. Needless to say, when we began cooking, we knew this was one dish we wanted to learn how to create at home, and we're so happy we did. Yet another family favorite we can share with you.

---

2 New York strip steaks (about 1½ pounds, or 681 g, total), thinly sliced

3 tablespoons (24 g) cornstarch

3 tablespoons (45 ml) vegetable oil, divided, plus more as needed

3 garlic cloves, minced

1 tablespoon (6 g) minced peeled fresh ginger

⅓ cup (80 ml) soy sauce

⅓ cup (80 ml) water

½ cup (113 g) packed brown sugar

Steamed rice for serving (preferably jasmine)

2 scallions, white and green parts, cut into 1-inch (2.5 cm) pieces

1 teaspoon toasted sesame seeds (optional)

1. Cut the sirloin into ⅛-inch (0.3 cm)-thick strips. Place them in a medium-size bowl, add the cornstarch, and mix well to evenly coat all of the steak.

2. Bring the griddle to medium-high heat.

3. Place a small saucepan over the heat and pour in 1 tablespoon (15 ml) of oil to heat. Add the garlic and ginger and sauté for about 1 minute—do not let the garlic brown. Add the soy sauce, water, and brown sugar. Cook, stirring, until the sauce comes to a rolling boil and the sugar dissolves.

4. While the sauce cooks, bring another section of the griddle to medium heat.

5. Pour 1 to 2 tablespoons (15 to 30 ml) of oil onto the griddle over medium heat and place the steak in the oil. Sear the first side for about 30 seconds. Flip the steak and cook for 1 minute. Pour the sauce over the steak and cook until the sauce thickens on the steak. Pull the steak off the griddle and serve over rice, garnished with scallions and sesame seeds (if using).

NAVAJO FRY BREAD TACOS

SERVES 6 TO 8

Do you have a "food memory" from childhood? We do, and it's these Navajo tacos. From a field trip in fourth grade, we had the amazing opportunity living in Utah to sink our teeth into our first Navajo tacos. From that day, we've been itching to develop a recipe that we could bring to the griddle, and here it is! Serve these delicious tacos topped as you like; we like diced tomato, pico de gallo, shredded lettuce, sliced black olives, and sour cream.

FOR FILLING:

2 tablespoons (30 ml) vegetable oil, divided

1 pound (454 g) 80/20 ground beef

¼ cup (36 g) taco seasoning

½ yellow onion, diced

1 (15-ounce, or 425 g) can dark red kidney beans, drained and rinsed

1 (14.5-ounce, or 410 g) can petite diced tomatoes, undrained

1 (4-ounce, or 115 g) can diced green chilies

FOR FRY BREAD:

2 cups (240 g) all-purpose flour, plus more for dusting

2½ teaspoons (13 g) baking powder

1 teaspoon salt

1 cup (240 ml) warm water

3 to 4 tablespoons (45 to 60 ml) vegetable oil

1. To make the filling: Bring the griddle to medium-low heat.

2. Pour 1 tablespoon (15 ml) of oil onto the griddle and place the ground beef in it. Cook, chopping the beef into very small pieces, until browned and no longer pink. Sprinkle on the taco seasoning and cook for 3 to 4 minutes more until the meat is properly seasoned.

3. Place a large skillet over medium-low heat and pour in 1 tablespoon (15 ml) of oil to heat. Add the onion and cook for 2 to 3 minutes, just until the onion begins to soften. Stir in the kidney beans, tomatoes and their juices, and chilies. Decrease the heat to low. Add the ground beef to the skillet and stir everything together, continuing to simmer. Keep the meat warm while you prepare the fry bread.

4. To make the fry bread: In a large bowl, combine the flour, baking powder, and salt. Add the warm water and mix using a fork until a dough forms. Lightly flour a clean work surface and turn the dough out onto it. Knead the dough for 5 minutes, then transfer to a clean bowl and cover tightly with plastic wrap. Let the dough rest for 10 minutes. Divide the dough into eight equal portions by pinching off golf ball–size balls of dough, then pat and roll the dough balls into roughly 6-inch (15 cm) disks on a lightly floured surface. Keep them covered with plastic wrap while you prepare to fry them.

5. To fry the bread: Bring the griddle to medium heat.

6. Pour 3 to 4 tablespoons (45 to 60 ml) of oil onto the griddle and heat until you see a wisp of white smoke. Place the fry bread in the hot oil. Cook until the bottom is golden brown, flip, and cook the second side to the same color. Continue to fry all the bread.

7. To assemble: Top the fry bread with the beef filling, piling it high, then top with your favorite toppings.

TOMAHAWK RIB-EYE STEAK

The steak of all steaks—and yes, this is the best we've ever made. We use this same process on every cut of steak, and even our pork chops, now. More people have told us how much they love this process, and how successful their cooks are, than any other cook we've shared. This one delivers!

---

1 (3-pound, or 1.3 kg) tomahawk rib-eye steak (about 2½ inches, or 6 cm, thick)

Salt and ground black pepper

Vegetable or olive oil

8 tablespoons (1 stick, or 112 g) garlic and herb butter (preferably Kerrygold)

1. Pull the steak from the refrigerator and let rest at room temperature for 30 minutes before cooking. Season all sides liberally with salt and pepper.

2. Bring one side of the griddle to high heat and the other side to medium to medium-low heat.

3. Pour a small amount of oil onto the high-heat side of the griddle and place the steak in the oil. Sear for 2 minutes, flip the steak, and sear the other side for 2 minutes (if your steak is thinner, sear it for 1 minute per side). Once both sides are seared, roll the edges on the heat to create a sear all the way around the steak.

4. Pour about 1 tablespoon (15 ml) of oil onto the medium to medium-low side of the griddle and add 1 tablespoon (14 g) of butter to melt. As the butter melts, place the steak on the butter and cook for 5 to 7 minutes, basting the steak with the juices coming from the steak and the butter. Check after 5 minutes—if the steak is adequately darkened, add 1 tablespoon (14 g) of butter to the griddle to melt, flip the steak, place it in the melted butter, and cook for 5 to 7 minutes, basting the steak with the juices and butter. Continue cooking the steak this way, adding more butter and flipping the steak every 5 minutes and basting, until the internal temperature reaches your desired doneness. Total cook time will be about 27 minutes (for 120°F to 125°F, or 49°C to 52°C).

5. Pull the steak off the griddle and let it rest for 5 to 10 minutes before slicing and serving.

BEEF STIR-FRY ON THE GRIDDLE

In the mood for amazing Asian cuisine? Look no further. This beef stir-fry will satisfy any craving. Marinating the meat the night before makes this one of the quickest cooks on the griddle! Look for sweet soy sauce at Asian markets. Serve with your favorite sides.

---

2 pounds (908 g) stir-fry beef

5 tablespoons (75 ml) sweet soy sauce, divided

3 tablespoons (45 ml) vegetable oil, divided

2 teaspoons salt

1 teaspoon ground black pepper

4 large eggs

1 (12-ounce, or 340 g) bag frozen vegetable stir-fry mix

1. In a shallow dish, combine the beef and 2 tablespoons (30 ml) of sweet soy sauce. Toss to coat well. Cover and refrigerate overnight.

2. Bring the griddle to medium-low heat.

3. Pour about 2 tablespoons (30 ml) of oil onto the griddle, then place the beef on it. Cook the beef until about halfway cooked through (some pink remains), then cover the beef with 2 tablespoons (30 ml) of sweet soy sauce and season with salt and pepper. Stir-fry the beef in the sauce for 2 to 3 minutes, then pull the beef to the cooler side of the griddle, not over direct heat.

4. Pour another 1 tablespoon (15 ml) of oil onto the griddle again. Crack the eggs into the oil and cook, scrambling, until almost cooked through, flip the eggs, and cook until fully cooked. Place the eggs on the beef.

5. Place the vegetables on the griddle (we preheat the vegetables in the microwave to make the cooking process quicker) and stir-fry for about 2 minutes, or until the vegetables are hot and cooked through. Pull the beef and eggs back onto the heat and mix all the ingredients together. Top everything with the remaining 1 tablespoon (15 ml) of sweet soy sauce and cook for 1 to 2 minutes before pulling off the griddle to serve.

BEEF & BROCCOLI

Though this dish may seem complex, it is so easy to get on the plate. Once you make it, you'll wonder why you waited so long to give it a try. We like serving this with jasmine rice to round out the meal.

---

1 tablespoon (15 ml) soy sauce

1 teaspoon sesame oil

2 teaspoons cornstarch, divided

1 teaspoon baking soda

1 pound (454 g) flank steak, sliced against the grain into ¼-inch (0.6 cm) or thinner strips

1 pound (454 g) fresh broccoli florets

⅓ cup (80 ml) beef broth or stock

¼ cup (60 ml) oyster sauce

2 tablespoons (30 ml) vegetable oil

2 garlic cloves, minced

1. In a small bowl, whisk the soy sauce, sesame oil, 1 teaspoon of cornstarch, and the baking soda to create the marinade.

2. Place the beef strips into a gallon (3.8 L)-size resealable plastic bag and pour the marinade over them. Seal the bag and refrigerate for at least 2 hours, or overnight for best results.

3. In a large microwave-safe bowl with a vented lid (or covered with plastic wrap with a few holes poked in to let steam escape), microwave the broccoli on high power for 1 to 2 minutes. Set aside.

4. In another small bowl, stir together the broth, oyster sauce, and remaining 1 teaspoon of cornstarch until the cornstarch is fully dissolved. Set aside.

5. Bring the griddle to medium heat.

6. Pour the vegetable oil onto the griddle and let heat until you see a wisp of white smoke. Toss the garlic into the hot oil and cook for about 30 seconds until fragrant.

7. Remove the meat from the marinade and toss it on the griddle. Discard the marinade. Cook the beef for 1 to 2 minutes, continually moving the beef so it browns on all sides but is still rare. Once the beef is seared, add the broccoli and cook for 1 minute. Stir in the sauce while stir-frying the beef and broccoli. Cook for about 1 minute until the sauce turns into a nice thick gravy, then pull the beef and broccoli off the griddle.

BEEF LO MEIN

Just like our fried rice, this lo mein recipe can be adapted to any protein! The difference is in which broth you prefer with the given protein. This one is all beef, and oh, so good!

FOR SAUCE:

¼ cup (60 ml) beef broth

3 tablespoons (45 ml) oyster sauce

1 tablespoon (15 ml) soy sauce

1 teaspoon cornstarch

1 teaspoon sesame oil

1 teaspoon Ac'cent Flavor Enhancer

FOR LO MEIN:

3 tablespoons (45 ml) vegetable oil,
    plus more as needed

4 teaspoons (11 g) grated peeled
    fresh ginger

2 teaspoons minced garlic

1 pound (454 g) top sirloin, cut into 1-inch
    (2.5 cm) pieces

½ carrot, julienned

4 ounces (115 g) baby bok choy, trimmed

1 (8-ounce, or 225 g) can water
    chestnuts, drained

1 (14-ounce, or 395 g) udon noodles

1. To make the sauce: In a small bowl, stir together the broth, oyster sauce, soy sauce, cornstarch, sesame oil, and Ac'cent until blended. Set aside.

2. Bring the griddle to medium heat.

3. To make the lo mein: Pour the vegetable oil onto the griddle and let heat until you see a wisp of white smoke. Add the ginger and garlic and cook for about 20 seconds until light brown and fragrant. Stir in the sirloin and cook for 2 to 3 minutes until it is about a medium doneness. Add the carrot, bok choy, water chestnuts, and noodles and cook for 3 minutes until all is well mixed.

4. Pour the sauce directly over the beef lo mein and incorporate it well into all the ingredients. Cook until the sauce starts to bubble and thicken. Transfer the lo mein to a serving platter and serve immediately.

SHALLOW-FRIED CHICKEN-FRIED STEAK

SERVES 2

Who knew frying breaded steak could be so much fun and absolutely delicious? Dig into chicken-fried steak from your griddle, and you'll never prepare this dish another way! Serve with Country Gravy (page 120) to add the finishing touch to this Southern favorite.

3 to 5 tablespoons (45 to 75 ml) vegetable oil

2 cups (240 g) all-purpose flour

Salt

2 teaspoons ground black pepper, divided

1 tablespoon (14g) seasoning salt

2 cups (480 ml) buttermilk

2 cube steaks (any size)

Country Gravy (below) for serving (optional)

1. Bring the griddle to medium heat. Pour the oil onto the griddle and heat until you see a wisp of white smoke.

2. While the griddle heats, in a shallow bowl, whisk the flour, salt to taste, 1 teaspoon of pepper, and seasoning salt to combine. Pour the buttermilk into another shallow bowl.

3. Place the steaks on a work surface and pound them to tenderize and flatten for quick and even cooking. Season with salt to taste and the remaining 1 teaspoon of pepper.

4. Dredge the steaks in the flour mixture, coating the entire steak and pressing the flour into the steak to ensure complete coverage. Dredge the steak in the buttermilk until completely covered, and then dredge it in the flour again, ensuring complete coverage. Lay the steak on the griddle in the hot oil. Cook until the internal temperature of the chicken reaches a minimum of 165°F (74°C), at least 8 to 10 minutes, flipping the steak every 2 minutes and watching to ensure the breading does not burn, until each side is golden brown.

COUNTRY GRAVY

SERVES 3 TO 4

This mouthwateringly good, buttery, savory country gravy will make you a true Southerner, no matter where you're from!

3 tablespoons (42 g) unsalted butter

3 tablespoons (22.5 g) all-purpose flour

3 cups (720 ml) whole milk

Salt and ground black pepper

1. Bring one side of the griddle to medium-high heat and place a medium-size pot onto the griddle, placing butter in the pot to melt. Once melted, pour in the flour, creating a roux (a cooked mixture of flour and fat used as a thickener in a soup or a sauce). Stir until the roux is pasty, then, still stirring to ensure the roux does not clump, slowly pour in 1 cup (240 ml) of milk and cook for 1 minute. Add in the remaining 1 cup (240 ml) of milk.

2. Season the gravy with salt and pepper to taste. Continue stirring and bring the gravy to a boil. Cook, continuing to stir until the gravy is to your desired thickness, lower the heat and let it cool slightly, then serve.

KOREAN-STYLE BARBECUE SHORT RIBS

SERVES 8

We have become such big fans of all of our Asian-style dishes because we can see that the ingredients work so well together. These Korean-style ribs prove this point. Serve these to your guests and they will not believe you made these—they are that good!

3 pounds (1.3 kg) beef short ribs, halved across the bone

⅓ cup (80 ml) soy sauce

⅓ cup (75 g) packed light brown sugar

½ cup (120 ml) rice wine

1 tablespoon (15 ml) sesame oil

2 teaspoons ground black pepper

¼ teaspoon gochujang

1 medium-size white onion, diced

1 to 2 teaspoons minced garlic

1 small Asian pear, peeled, cored, and diced

1-inch (2.5 cm) piece fresh ginger, peeled and chopped

2 tablespoons (30 ml) vegetable oil

2 teaspoons sesame seeds

Steamed rice for serving

Large lettuce leaves for serving

1. Pat the short ribs dry with a paper towel and place them in a shallow bowl or a gallon (3.8 L)-size resealable plastic bag.

2. In a medium-size bowl, whisk the soy sauce, brown sugar, rice wine, sesame oil, pepper, and gochujang to blend.

3. In a food processor, combine the onion, garlic, pear, and ginger and process until puréed. Add the purée to the soy sauce mixture and stir until all ingredients are well combined. Pour the marinade over the ribs, cover (or seal), and refrigerate for at least 2 hours, or overnight for best results. Bring to room temperature before cooking.

4. Bring the griddle to medium heat.

5. Pour the vegetable oil onto the griddle. Remove the ribs from the marinade and place them in the oil. Discard the marinade. Cook for about 4 minutes, flip the ribs, and cook for about 4 minutes more until the internal temperature reaches 140°F (60°C). Transfer the ribs to a plate and sprinkle with sesame seeds. Serve hot with steamed rice and lettuce leaves

DOUBLE TACO GOODNESS

We love everything in double form . . . we are twins, after all. So, how do you make a taco even better? You double it up, and make a double-decker taco!

---

1 (16-ounce, or 454 g) can refried beans

1 to 2 tablespoons (15 to 30 ml) vegetable oil

1 pound (454 g) 80/20 ground beef

1 (1-ounce, or 28 g) packet taco seasoning

12 (6-inch, or 15 cm) taco-size flour tortillas

12 hard taco shells

1 (15-ounce, or 425 g) jar cheese sauce/ queso dip

1 (8-ounce, or 225 g) bag shredded iceberg lettuce

1 medium-size tomato, diced

1 cup (115 g) shredded Mexican-style cheese blend

Sour cream for serving

1. Bring the griddle to medium to medium-low heat.

2. In a small pot, heat the refried beans on one side of the griddle to warm up. In another pot, heat the oil. Add the ground beef to the hot oil and cook until browned, finely chopping the meat as you cook it. Pour the taco seasoning over the meat and mix until all the beef is covered, then remove the beef from the griddle and place in a medium-size bowl.

3. Place 1 flour tortilla on a work surface. Spread some of the warmed refried beans over the tortilla, out to the edges. Place a hard taco shell in the middle and wrap the flour tortilla around it, pressing it to the hard shell so it sticks.

4. Place a second flour tortilla on a work surface and spread some of the cheese sauce over it, out to the edges. Place a hard taco shell in the middle and wrap the flour tortilla around it, pressing it to the hard shell so it sticks.

5. Repeat steps 3 and 4 until all the tortillas and taco shells are pressed together with either the refried beans or cheese sauce.

6. Fill each tortilla with ground beef. Top each with lettuce, tomato, shredded cheese, and a dollop of sour cream to serve.

CARNE ASADA STREET TACOS*

When someone asks you to make tacos for dinner, this is a great way to take it over the top! Carne asada street tacos will have your family convinced you are a five-star chef!

2 tablespoons (30 ml) soy sauce

2 tablespoons (30 ml) freshly squeezed lime juice

2 tablespoons (30 ml) vegetable oil, divided

3 garlic cloves, minced

2 teaspoons chili powder

½ teaspoon ground cumin

1 teaspoon oregano

1½ pounds (681 g) skirt steak, cut into ½-inch (1 cm) pieces

12 (4½-inch, or 11 cm) street-size taco flour tortillas, or (8-inch, or 20 cm) corn tortillas, or a mix, warmed

Shredded cheese of choice for topping (optional)

1 cup (160 g) diced red onion

½ cup (8 g) chopped fresh cilantro

Creamy Jalapeño Ranch Dressing (see Chicken Street Tacos, page 71) for topping (optional)

2 limes, cut into wedges

1. In a medium-size bowl, whisk the soy sauce, lime juice, 1 tablespoon (15 ml) of oil, the garlic, chili powder, cumin, and oregano to blend. Pour the marinade into a gallon (3.8 L)-size resealable plastic bag and add the steak. Seal the bag, turning to coat the steak. Refrigerate to marinate for 3 hours, or up to overnight for the best flavor, but no longer than 12 hours.

2. Bring the griddle to medium-low heat.

3. Pour the remaining 1 tablespoon (15 ml) of oil onto the griddle. Let heat until you see a wisp of white smoke, then add the steak and marinade to the hot oil and cook for 5 to 7 minutes, stirring often, until the steak is browned and the marinade is reduced.

4. Fill the warmed tortillas with the steak, cheese (if using), onion, cilantro, and a drizzle of ranch (if using). Finish with a squeeze or two of lime juice.

*Adapted from Chungah Rhee, Damn Good Recipes: damndelicious.net/2019/04/18/mexican-street-tacos/

EVERYTHING TACOS

One of the best parts of having a cooking show on YouTube is the many recipe and cook ideas that pour in! Such was the case with these Everything Tacos (or Cowboy Tacos). Viewer Joe E. shared this flavor-popping recipe, and wow, are we happy he did. Plus, the recipe easily scales up or down based on how many cowhands you're feeding. Add some shredded cheese, your favorite hot sauce, and some salsa to the toppings list, or anything else you like.

---

1 pound (454 g) skirt steak, thinly sliced against the grain

1 tablespoon (6 g) beef bouillon powder

1 pound (454 g) lean boneless pork or boneless, skinless chicken breast, chopped

Salt and ground black pepper

Garlic powder

1 pound (454 g) bacon, chopped into ½-inch (1 cm) pieces

1 pound (454 g) potatoes, cubed

2 chorizo sausage links

3 jalapeño peppers or serrano peppers (if you like it spicy), sliced

1 or 2 yellow or white onions, diced

8 (10-inch , 25 cm) burrito-size or 12 (6-inch , 15 cm) taco-size flour tortillas, warmed

1 or 2 tomatoes, diced

Chopped fresh cilantro for garnish

1. Bring the griddle to medium-low heat, leaving one side off to use as a warming area.

2. Season the steak with the bouillon powder. Season the pork with salt, pepper, and garlic powder to taste. Set aside.

3. Cook the bacon on the griddle, flipping, until it is cooked to your desired crispiness. Move the bacon to a cooler side of the griddle, not over direct heat, leaving the grease where it is.

4. Place the potatoes in the bacon grease, season with salt and pepper, and cook, stirring, until browned and cooked through. Move the potatoes to the cooler side of the griddle.

5. Throw the chorizo on the griddle, then the steak and pork. Cook for about 7 minutes, turning, or until the internal temperature of the chorizo reaches at least 160°F (71°C), the pork reaches 145°F (63°C), and the steak is cooked to your desired doneness. Move the cooked meats to the cooler side of the griddle.

6. Toss on the jalapeños and onions. Cook for 2 to 3 minutes until the vegetables begin to soften but are not cooked all the way through. Mix everything together and cook for 3 to 5 minutes, stirring, so the flavors blend.

7. Serve with the warm tortillas, tomatoes, and cilantro to garnish and any other toppings you fancy.

CONEY ISLAND DOGS

MAKES 6 HOT DOGS

Another day, another recommendation, another "copycat" cook. This was one of the first hot dog recipes we tried on the griddle, and it made us huge fans of cooking dogs this way. This sauce is supreme and we won't make it any other way.

---

8 ounces (225 g) 80/20 ground beef

1 (8-ounce, or 225 g) can tomato sauce

2¼ teaspoons (34 ml) Worcestershire sauce

2 tablespoons (30 g) brown sugar

1 tablespoon (15 ml) freshly squeezed lemon juice

¾ teaspoon chili powder

2 tablespoons (12.5 g) chopped celery

½ cup chopped onion (80 g), divided

Salt

6 hot dogs

6 hot dog buns

Mustard for topping

1. Bring two separate sides of the griddle to medium-low heat.

2. On one side, begin browning the ground beef.

3. While the beef cooks, in a medium-size skillet on the other side of the griddle, combine the tomato sauce, Worcestershire sauce, brown sugar, lemon juice, and chili powder. Bring to a boil, stirring occasionally (if it is taking too long, bring the heat up to medium).

4. Once the ground beef is almost browned, add the celery and ¼ cup (40 g) of onion to the ground beef and season to taste with salt. Cook the meat until it is completely browned, then add it and the vegetables to the sauce. Cook for 10 to 20 minutes to allow the flavors to marry, stirring occasionally.

5. Place the hot dogs on the griddle and cook them to your preference.

6. Build your Coney Island dog by putting the hot dog in the bun, topping it with mustard, then Coney sauce, and finally some of the remaining chopped onion.

CALIFORNIA BURRITOS WITH AVOCADO CREMA

SERVES 4

If ever there were a more "American-ized" burrito than the California burrito with the inclusion of french fries, we have yet to find it! This burrito combines so many of our favorite flavors, it really stands out as a classic "banger!" Note: We use an air fryer to cook the fries for this dish, but you can cook them however you prefer.

FOR SPICE MIX:

1 tablespoon (7 g) ground cumin

1 tablespoon (9 g) garlic powder

2 teaspoons smoked paprika

1 teaspoon salt

1 teaspoon chili powder

1 teaspoon onion powder

½ teaspoon ground black pepper

FOR MARINADE AND STEAK:

⅓ cup (80 ml) soy sauce

⅓ cup (80 ml) freshly squeezed orange juice

2 tablespoons (30 ml) freshly squeezed lime juice

2 tablespoons (30 ml) olive oil

1½ tablespoons (23 g) brown sugar

1 teaspoon liquid smoke

1½ pounds (681 g) flank steak

4 tablespoons vegetable oil, divided, for cooking

1. To make the spice mix: In a small bowl, stir together all the spice mix ingredients until evenly blended. Reserve 3 tablespoons (28 g) for the marinade in step 2, and store any remaining spice mix in an airtight container for another use.

2. To make the marinade and steak: In a medium-size bowl, whisk the soy sauce, orange juice, reserved spice mix, lime juice, olive oil, brown sugar, and liquid smoke until well blended. Place the steak in a large resealable plastic bag and pour in the marinade. Seal the bag, turning to coat the steak and ensuring all parts are covered with the liquid. Refrigerate for at least 4 hours, or up to 24 hours.

3. To cook the steak: Bring one side of the griddle to medium-high heat and another section to medium-low heat.

4. Pour 2 tablespoons (30 ml) of vegetable oil onto the griddle over medium-high heat.

5. Remove the steak from the marinade and place it in the oil over medium-high heat. Discard the marinade. Sear for 2 minutes per side.

6. Pour 2 tablespoons (30 ml) of vegetable oil onto the griddle over medium-low heat and pull the steak to the cooler side. Cook for 7 minutes per side. Continue to cook and flip for 3 to 5 minutes per side until the steak is cooked to your liking (total cook time for medium-rare is about 18 minutes). Pull the steak off the griddle, wrap it in aluminum foil, and let rest for 20 minutes. Remove the foil and thinly slice the steak against the grain.

7. To make the fries: We use the air fryer to cook these fries. While the steak rests, bring a large pot full of water to a boil. Add the fries and boil for 2 minutes. Using tongs, transfer the fries to paper towels to drain. Pat dry with additional paper towels. Transfer the fries to a large bowl, pour in the vegetable oil, and toss to coat.

FOR FRIES:

2 large russet potatoes, cut into french fry strips as thick or thin as you like

1 tablespoon (15 ml) vegetable oil

Salt

FOR BURRITOS:

4 to 6 (10-inch, or 25 cm) burrito-size flour tortillas, warmed

Avocado Crema (below) for serving

Pico de gallo for serving

Shredded cheese of choice for serving

8. Preheat the air fry to 400°F (200°C).

9. Place the fries in the air fry basket and into the air fryer. Cook for 10 minutes. Check the fries and toss the basket to redistribute and keep them from sticking. Cook for 10 minutes more, checking and tossing every 5 minutes, until crispy and browned. Lightly season the hot fries with salt.

10. To build the burritos: Place the warmed tortillas on a work surface. Spread a layer of avocado crema over the tortillas. Top each with steak slices, followed by pico de gallo and a handful of fries. Top all that with cheese (or anything else you wish!). Fold in both sides of the tortilla, over the filling, then roll up the burrito from the bottom snugly around the filling. Serve and enjoy!

AVOCADO CREMA*

3 CUPS (675 G)

This is something we didn't know we needed, and now we can't live without. Any time a dish calls for avocado, or even guacamole, we first check to see if this crema will suffice—it is THAT good.

---

*Adapted from a recipe created by Jennifer on her *Carlsbad Cravings* blog.

2 large avocados

1 cup (240 g) sour cream

¼ cup (60 g) mayonnaise

2 tablespoons (30 ml) freshly squeezed lime juice

½ teaspoon salt

½ teaspoon ground cumin

½ teaspoon garlic powder

Halve and pit the avocados. Using a spoon, scoop the avocado flesh from the halves into a medium-size bowl. Add the remaining crema ingredients and mash and mix with a fork until everything is blended together creating a soft cream. Cover and refrigerate until needed.

CHEESESTEAK QUESADILLAS

We have learned that shaved rib eye can serve many purposes—as long as it's in the form of a "cheesesteak!" We sometimes can't decide which we like better: the hoagie, the tortilla, the egg roll, or, OKAY, we love them ALL! The buttery-ness on these quesadillas is tough to beat! You have to try this one!

3 tablespoons (45 ml) vegetable oil, divided

2 tablespoons (28 g) unsalted butter, plus more for the tortillas

1 large yellow onion, diced

1 green bell pepper, diced

2 teaspoons salt, divided

2 teaspoons ground black pepper, divided

1 pound (454 g) rib eye, shaved or as thinly sliced as possible

8 (6-inch, or 15 cm) taco-size flour tortillas

12 slices provolone cheese

Favorite dipping sauce for serving

1. Bring the griddle to medium-low heat.

2. Pour 1 tablespoon (15 ml) of oil onto the griddle, then place the butter on it to melt. Lay the onion in the melted butter, followed by the green pepper, and add 1 teaspoon of salt and 1 teaspoon of pepper. Cook for 5 to 6 minutes, moving the vegetables slowly, until the onion begins to turn translucent. Move the vegetables to a cooler side of the griddle, not over direct heat, or set aside off the griddle.

3. Pour the remaining 2 tablespoons (30 ml) of oil onto the griddle and lay the rib eye flat in it, spreading it out. Season with the remaining 1 teaspoon of salt and 1 teaspoon of pepper. Cook for 1 to 2 minutes to create a sear. Once the meat begins to turn brown, indicating it is cooked through, stir and chop the rib eye with a scraper to break up the meat. Mix the cooked rib eye with the onion and pepper and set aside.

4. Clean a space on the griddle to cook the quesadillas. Spread butter on one side of each tortilla. Lay four tortillas on the griddle and build the quesadilla by laying a generous amount of the steak and vegetables onto the tortilla (ensuring equal parts for all quesadillas). Place three slices of provolone over the rib eye on each and place a second tortilla on top, butter-side up. Cook the quesadillas until the bottom tortilla is golden brown, carefully flip the tortilla with a spatula, and continue cooking until the cheese is melted and the bottom tortilla is golden brown. Pull the tortillas from the heat and cut into quarters to serve with your favorite dipping sauce.

GRILLED CHEESE BURRITOS

What started out as a "Taco Bell copycat" recipe has turned not only into a family favorite but also a cook that brings everyone together. These burritos are highly requested by the kids and their friends—and it is always a good time.

---

1 (5.6-ounce, or 159 g) package Spanish or Mexican rice

2 tablespoons (30 ml) vegetable oil

1 pound (454 g) 80/20 ground beef

1 (1-ounce, or 28 g) packet taco seasoning

6 to 8 (10-inch, or 25 cm) burrito-size flour tortillas

1 (15-ounce, or 425 g) jar cheese sauce/ queso dip

1 to 2 pounds (454 to 908 g) shredded cheese of choice

Sour cream for serving

1 large tomato, cut into slices

1. Cook the rice according to the package directions. Keep warm.

2. Bring the griddle to medium-low heat.

3. Pour the oil onto the griddle and place the ground beef in it. Cook for 4 to 5 minutes, breaking up the meat, until brown. Season the beef with the taco seasoning, cook for 3 to 4 minutes, mixing it in, then pull the ground beef off the heat.

4. Place the tortillas on the griddle for 30 seconds to 1 minute to warm. Once warmed, transfer to a work surface and build the burritos: Spread the tortillas with a layer of queso dip, followed by ground beef, cheese, a few dollops of sour cream, rice, and tomato slices. Fold in the sides and firmly roll up the burritos.

5. On a cleared area of the griddle, lay down a strip of shredded cheese, the length of a burrito, and place the first burrito directly onto the cheese. Cook for about 1 minute, or until the cheese is melted onto the tortilla. Create a second strip of cheese on the griddle in front of the burrito. Using a scraper or sturdy spatula, flip the burrito so the top side is now resting on the second layer of cheese. Cook for about 1 minute until the cheese melts onto the burrito. Pull and place on a plate for serving. Repeat with the remaining burritos and shredded cheese.

PORK &
SAUSAGE

AMAZIN' SPICY PORK BELLY SANDWICHES

This recipe was shared with us by our great friend Matthew A. from New York. He uses the sauce for just about everything, so we decided to use it for some incredible tasty pork belly sandwiches!

½ **cup (120 ml) soy sauce**

¼ **cup (80 g) honey**

¼ **cup (60 ml) sriracha**

2 **tablespoons (30 ml) vegetable oil**

8 **ounces (225 g) pork belly, ¼ inch (0.6 cm) thick, halved lengthwise**

1 **to 2 tablespoons (15 to 30 g) mayonnaise**

2 **sandwich buns**

½ **cup (110 g) prepared Asian-style coleslaw**

1. Bring the griddle to medium heat.

2. In a medium-size saucepan, whisk the soy sauce, honey, and sriracha to blend. Place the pan over medium heat and bring the glaze to a rolling boil. Cook for 15 minutes to let the sauce reduce and thicken. Keep warm.

3. Bring another section of the griddle to low heat.

4. Pour the oil onto the griddle over low heat and place the pork belly in it. Cook for about 4 minutes, flip the pork belly, and cook for 4 minutes more. Continue flipping and cooking the pork for about 16 minutes total (slow cooking the pork belly gives the fat time to render, giving it more flavor). Transfer the cooked pork belly to the glaze and let it warm in the sauce for 7 minutes, turning occasionally. Halve each piece of pork widthwise (for four pieces total).

5. Spread a thin layer of mayo on the cut sides of the buns. Top each bottom bun with a generous spoonful of coleslaw, then two pieces of pork belly "crisscrossed" and the top bun. Serve the extra glaze on the side for dipping.

HAWAIIAN FRIED RICE

If we had to pick a "favorite" fried rice, this is it! It's kind of like picking a favorite child, though we love them all for different reasons. That said, it's still our favorite (just don't tell the others)! We also do this one with a "twist," using either our homemade teriyaki sauce or Mr. Yoshida's Sweet & Savory Marinade and Sauce. Note: You do need to cook and cool the rice ahead; overnight is best, so keep that in mind when planning for this dish.

---

4 cups (800 g) jasmine rice

4 tablespoons (60 ml) vegetable oil, divided

2 garlic cloves, minced

8 tablespoons (1 stick, or 112 g) unsalted butter

2 to 3 teaspoons (15 ml) sesame oil

1 (12-ounce, or 340 g) bag mixed frozen veggies (corn, peas, carrots)

½ medium-size yellow onion, diced

4 large eggs

2 (8-ounce, or 225 g) packages cooked ham cubes

1 cup (240 ml) Teriyaki Marinade (see Teriyaki Chicken Sandwiches, page 69) or Mr. Yoshida's Sweet & Savory Marinade and Sauce)

1 pineapple, cut into 1-inch (2.5 cm) chunks

1 to 2 tablespoons (8 to 16 g) sesame seeds

1. Cook the rice according to the package directions. Spread it out on a baking sheet and refrigerate, on the sheet, overnight to cool and dry.

2. Bring the griddle to medium-low heat.

3. Pour 2 tablespoons (30 ml) of vegetable oil onto the griddle and place the garlic and butter in the oil, immediately followed by the rice. Cook the rice for 5 to 7 minutes, stirring and mixing. Mix in the sesame oil.

4. On a separate area of the griddle, also over medium-low heat, pour on 1 tablespoon (15 ml) of oil and add the vegetables and onion to it.

5. While the vegetables cook, place the remaining 1 table-spoon (15 ml) of oil next to the rice and crack the eggs into the oil. Once the eggs begin to cook, lightly scramble them for a minute or two, then mix the eggs into the rice.

6. Once the vegetables are hot and cooked, move them to a section of the griddle that is no longer on to keep warm.

7. Place the ham cubes on the griddle where the vegetables were. Because they are already cooked, we just want to heat them up and get a light crisp on the pieces. Pour 1 tablespoon (15 ml) of teriyaki marinade on the ham and lay the pineapple next to the ham, adding 1 tablespoon (15 ml) of marinade to the pineapple as well. Cook for 1 to 2 minutes and then combine the ham and pineapple with the vegetables, then mix everything with the rice and eggs. Add more marinade to the fried rice until you like how it tastes, sprinkle with sesame seeds, and enjoy!

SOUTHERN-STYLE PORK CHOPS

SERVES 2

We didn't grow up in the South, but the first time we made these pork chops, we wished we had. Serve these with your favorite Southern side dish, and you'll truly understand the very definition of "comfort food."

2 cups (240 g) all-purpose flour

2 tablespoons (24 g) Waltwins Usual Suspects Seasoning (page 52), plus more for seasoning the pork

2 cups (480 ml) buttermilk

2 large bone-in pork chops

3 to 5 tablespoons (45 to 75 ml) vegetable oil

1. Bring the griddle to medium-low heat.

2. While the griddle heats, in a shallow bowl, whisk the flour and Usual Suspects Seasoning to blend. Pour the buttermilk into another shallow bowl. Season the chops on both sides with the Usual Suspects Seasoning. Place each pork chop in the flour mix, coating the entire chop and pressing the flour into the chop to ensure complete coverage. Dredge the pork chops in the buttermilk until completely covered, and then coat them in the flour again, ensuring complete coverage.

3. Pour the oil onto the griddle to create a shallow-fry area and let it heat until you see a wisp of white smoke.

4. Lay the pork chops in the hot oil. Cook for 15 to 17 minutes, flipping the chops every 2 minutes, until each side is golden brown and watching to ensure the breading does not burn. When the chops' internal temperature reaches 145°F (63°C), pull them off the griddle. Let rest for 5 minutes before serving.

CUBAN-STYLE MARINATED PORK

From Adam's first-ever trip to Miami, Cuban sandwiches have been one of his personal favorites, so is it any surprise they are also Brett's favorite? With his mother-in-law being from Cuba, Adam learned this amazing recipe for marinated pork, and it has been our go-to for all Cuban pork dishes, especially Cuban (pressed) Sandwiches (page 144). Note: We depart from the griddle to cook the pork.

½ cup (120 ml) freshly squeezed orange juice

½ cup (120 ml) freshly squeezed lime juice

7 garlic cloves, minced

2 tablespoons (30 ml) extra-virgin olive oil

1½ teaspoons salt

1 teaspoon ground cumin

1 teaspoon dried oregano

⅛ teaspoon ground black pepper

1 (3-pound, or 1.3 kg) boneless pork shoulder roast

1. In a gallon (3.8 L)-size or larger resealable plastic bag, combine the orange and lime juices, garlic, oil, salt, cumin, oregano, and pepper. Add the roast, seal the bag, and turn the bag to coat the pork. Refrigerate for at least 6 hours to marinate and up to 24 hours.

2. Remove the pork from the marinade and place it in a slow cooker. Discard the marinade. Cover and cook on medium-low heat for 5 to 7 hours, or until the pork is fork-tender and falls apart easily.

GLAZED PORK BELLY

Seemingly inconspicuous, this pork belly and glaze cook became a memorable one, simply because the flavor was outstanding! We always know how good a cook is when, days later, we are still talking about it.

¼ **cup (80 g) honey**

¼ **cup (60 ml) soy sauce**

2 **tablespoons (30 ml) oyster sauce**

2 **teaspoons minced garlic**

2 **pounds (908 g) pork belly, cut into ¼- to ½-inch (0.6 to 1 cm)-thick slices**

Salt

1. In a small bowl, stir together the honey, soy sauce, oyster sauce, and garlic until blended.

2. Bring the griddle to medium-low heat.

3. Place the pork belly slices on the griddle and season liberally with salt. Cook for 2 to 3 minutes until the pork begins to brown. Turn each piece, season with salt, and cook for 2 to 3 minutes more to brown. Continue cooking and flipping until each piece is browned and cooked as desired.

4. Brush the pork with the glaze. Flip the pork belly and brush the other side with glaze. Cook for 2 to 3 minutes to help the glaze caramelize—but not burn! Pull the pork off the griddle and serve.

FRIED BOLOGNA SANDWICHES

What can be said here? You take a classic meat, fry it up, place your favorite toppings on it, and voilà, you've got an incredible sandwich that transformed the bologna sandwich you grew up on into a new homemade deli favorite!

FOR RED WINE VINAIGRETTE:

3 tablespoons (45 ml) red wine vinegar

1 tablespoon (15 ml) extra-virgin olive oil

2 to 3 teaspoons (12 g) Waltwins Usual
    Suspects Seasoning (page 52)

FOR SANDWICHES:

4 slices angus beef bologna (¼ inch,
    or 0.6 cm, thick)

2 tablespoons (30 ml) vegetable oil

8 slices American cheese

Mayonnaise for toasting and serving

4 slices artisan bread

Mustard for serving

1 large white onion, cut into rings

1 large tomato, cut into slices

Salt and ground black pepper

Dill pickle chips for serving

Sliced mild banana peppers for serving

1. To make the vinaigrette: In a medium-size bowl, whisk the vinegar, oil, and Usual Suspects Seasoning to blend. The oil and vinegar will separate, so whisking before use is key.

2. Bring the griddle to medium heat.

3. To make the sandwiches: While the griddle heats up, score the bologna edges with four cuts per slice to prevent curling.

4. Pour the oil onto the griddle and let heat until you see a wisp of white smoke. Place the bologna slices on the griddle. Cook for 1 to 2 minutes, or until the slices have a nice dark crust, then flip the bologna slices over. Place two slices of cheese on each bologna slice and cook for 1 to 2 minutes until the second side has a nice dark crust and the cheese melts.

5. While the cheese melts, spread mayo on both sides of each slice of bread and place them on the griddle. Cook until both sides are lightly browned and toasted as desired. Spread more mayo on one side of two pieces of toast and spread mustard on one side of the remaining two pieces of toast.

6. Pull the bologna off the griddle and place two slices on each of the mayo toasts. Top with onion and tomato, season with salt and pepper to taste, then add pickles and banana peppers. Whisk the vinaigrette and season the sandwiches with it to taste. Top the sandwich with the mustard toasts and enjoy.

PORK FRIED RICE

We weren't kidding when we said we absolutely love making fried rice! Growing up, whenever we grabbed fried rice at a local Chinese takeout place, it was always ham fried or pork fried rice. This adaptation with fresh pork makes one even better than takeout. Look for sweet soy sauce at Asian markets. Note: You do need to cook and cool the rice ahead; overnight is best, so keep that in mind when planning for this dish.

---

4 cups (800 g) jasmine rice

7 tablespoons (105 ml) vegetable oil, divided

2 garlic cloves, minced

8 tablespoons (1 stick, or 112 g) unsalted butter

2 to 3 teaspoons (15 ml) sesame oil

1 (16-ounce, or 454 g) bag mixed frozen vegetables (corn, peas, carrots)

½ medium-size yellow onion, diced

4 large eggs

2 pounds (908 g) boneless pork loin, cut into bite-size cubes

Sweet soy sauce or regular soy sauce

2 teaspoons salt

1 teaspoon ground black pepper

1 to 2 tablespoons (8 to 16 g) sesame seeds

1. Cook the rice according to the package directions. Spread it out on a baking sheet and refrigerate, on the sheet, overnight to cool and dry.

2. Bring the griddle to medium-low heat.

3. Pour about 2 tablespoons (30 ml) of vegetable oil onto the griddle. Place the garlic and butter in the oil, immediately followed by the rice. Stir-fry the rice in the garlic butter for 5 to 7 minutes. Mix in the sesame oil.

4. On a separate area of the griddle over medium-low heat, pour about 2 tablespoons (30 ml) of vegetable oil onto the surface and lay down the mixed vegetables and onion.

5. While the vegetables cook, pour 1 tablespoon (15 ml) of vegetable oil onto the griddle next to the rice and crack the eggs into the oil. Once the eggs begin to cook, lightly scramble them for a minute or two, then mix the eggs into the rice.

6. Once the vegetables are hot and cooked, move them to a section of the griddle that is no longer on to keep warm (or remove from the griddle if you need room to cook the pork).

7. Pour about 2 tablespoons (30 ml) of vegetable oil onto the griddle where the vegetables were and place the pork in it. Stir-fry the pork until browned and no longer pink.

8. While the pork cooks, season the rice and eggs, vegetables, and pork with the sweet soy sauce to taste and salt and pepper. Once the pork is cooked through, combine it with the vegetables and rice. Taste and season with more soy sauce, as needed, and sprinkle with sesame seeds to serve.

ITALIAN SAUSAGE, ONION & PEPPER HOAGIES

We have good friends to thank for requesting Italian sausage, peppers, and onions, which allowed us to do some research. The outcome of that research is this fabulous sandwich you are about to hold in your hands. You're welcome.

---

1 large yellow onion, cut into ¼-inch (0.6 cm) half-moons

1 green bell pepper, cut into 2- to 3-inch (5 to 7.5 cm)-long strips

1 red bell pepper, cut into 2- to 3-inch (5 to 7.5 cm)-long strips

1 yellow-orange bell pepper, cut into 2- to 3-inch (5 to 7.5 cm)-long strips

1 tablespoon (15 ml) balsamic vinegar

Salt and ground black pepper

3 tablespoons (45 ml) extra-virgin olive oil, divided

4 to 6 mild Italian sausage links

2 teaspoons minced garlic

1 (15-ounce, or 425 g) can diced tomatoes or crushed tomatoes

1 tablespoon (3 g) dried oregano

4 to 6 hoagie rolls, split

1. In a large bowl, combine the onion; green, red, and yellow bell peppers; vinegar; and salt and pepper to taste. Toss to coat and let sit for 30 minutes.

2. Bring the griddle to medium-low heat.

3. Pour 2 tablespoons (30 ml) of oil onto the griddle and place the sausages in the oil. Cook for about 20 minutes, turning the sausages frequently and ensuring even browning (do not sear). Move the sausages to a cooler side of the griddle, not over direct heat.

4. Pour the remaining 1 tablespoon (15 ml) of oil onto the griddle and add the garlic. Cook for 30 seconds. Add the marinated onion and bell peppers and the tomatoes. Sprinkle with the oregano. Cook for 2 to 3 minutes, mixing, until the vegetables are hot and evenly mixed.

5. Bring the sausages into the veggies and cook for 3 to 5 minutes. If you like, cut each sausage into ½-inch (1 cm) rounds and sear some of the edges on the griddle. Pull the sausages and vegetables off the griddle and serve in hoagie rolls.

CUBAN SANDWICHES

Another notch on our cooking cap! When I first sank my teeth into a Cuban sandwich in Miami as a teen, I only remember thinking two things: "Wow, this bread is really hard," and "Why do all of these flavors work so well together?!" Since learning to make Cuban sandwiches ourselves, we have learned to press these to perfection, creating a crispy, not overly hard, bread with a flavor that impresses everyone!

---

8 slices deli ham

2 tablespoons (22g) yellow mustard

4 Cuban rolls, halved horizontally

1 pound (454 g) cooked Cuban-Style Marinated Pork (page 137), shredded

8 slices Swiss cheese

Pickle chips for the sandwiches and serving

1. Bring the griddle to medium-low heat.

2. Place the ham on the griddle, heating each side for 30 seconds to 1 minute.

3. Spread a thin layer of mustard on the insides of the Cuban rolls. Layer a generous amount of pork on the bottom half of the roll. Place two slices of ham on the pork on each sandwich, followed by two slices of Swiss cheese. Top each sandwich with pickle chips (as many or as few as you like). Place the top roll on the sandwiches and place the sandwiches on the griddle. Using a press or a sturdy spatula, press down firmly on each sandwich, holding the press for 2 to 3 minutes, or until the bottom roll is toasted. Gently flip the sandwich and continue the process. The sandwich will flatten considerably as it is pressed. Slice the sandwich diagonally, nearly corner to corner, and serve!

WALTWINS HOMEMADE RIB SANDWICHES

When McDonald's first introduced its rib sandwich, Adam and Brett both became self-proclaimed "McRibbies"—or, hard-core McRib fans, chasing this favorite every year! This homemade rib sandwich may not taste like the original, but that is only because with pure thick-cut meat and fresh ingredients, this is really the next level of rib sandwiches.

---

2 cups (500 g) favorite barbecue sauce

1 tablespoon (15 ml) soy sauce

1 tablespoon (15 g) brown sugar

2 teaspoons Waltwins Usual Suspects Seasoning (page 52)

1 teaspoon Worcestershire sauce

1 pound (454 g) boneless country-style ribs

4 sub or hoagie rolls

1. In a large bowl, whisk the barbecue sauce, soy sauce, brown sugar, Usual SuspectsSeasoning, and Worcestershire sauce until combined. Place the ribs in the marinade, turning to ensure they are completely covered. Refrigerate for at least 1 hour.

2. Bring the griddle to medium to medium-low heat.

3. Remove the ribs from the marinade and place the ribs on the grill. Discard the marinade, and cook for 3 to 4 minutes per side, watching carefully to ensure they do not burn. Continue cooking and flipping for about 15 minutes more (20 to 25 minutes total), or until the internal temperature of the meat reaches 145°F (63°C). Pull the ribs off the griddle and let cool slightly before stuffing into a roll and into your belly!

BISCUITS & GRAVY

SERVES 4

Hands down, our favorite breakfast is biscuits and gravy. Adam always wanted to perfect a sausage gravy, and this trick our sister taught us to make a simple roux was just the ticket! Note: You will need a wire rack to cook the biscuits on the griddle surface.

---

3 tablespoons (42 g) unsalted butter, divided

8 frozen buttermilk biscuits

2 tablespoons (15 g) all-purpose flour

2 cups (480 ml) whole milk

1 pound (454 g) pork sausage (preferably Jimmy Dean's)

1. Bring one side of the griddle to medium-low heat.

2. Place 1 tablespoon (14 g) of butter on the griddle to melt and place the frozen biscuits on the butter. Cook for 1 to 2 minutes until the bottom of the biscuits is golden brown. Flip and cook for about 1 minute, or until the second side is golden brown. Once all the biscuits are browned, pull them from the direct heat and place on a wire rack on the griddle. If possible, cover with a dome and continue to cook the biscuits while making the gravy.

3. Bring a section of the griddle to medium-high heat and place a large pan or skillet on it, leaving the section at medium-low on. Place the remaining 2 tablespoons (28 g) of butter in the pan to melt. Once the butter is melted and begins to bubble, slowly stir in the flour. Once all the flour is mixed evenly (no clumps), slowly pour in the milk while stirring.

4. While monitoring the gravy, cook the sausage on the griddle over medium-low heat, breaking it up while cooking until browned and cooked through. The sausage consistency should be like "chunky" ground beef with some smaller pieces and some medium-size ground pork pieces.

5. When the gravy is boiling and the sausage is cooked, add the sausage to the gravy and boil until it reduces to the consistency you like.

6. Split the biscuits. Place two biscuits per serving onto plates, cut-side up, and top with sausage gravy.

FRESH FISH
& SEAFOOD

SHRIMP STIR-FRY

SERVES 4

Need an excuse to make another mouthwatering Asian-inspired dish, or just another shrimp recipe? Say no more. We understand. We absolutely love this stir-fry sauce, and it makes this recipe another restaurant-quality cook for your griddle. Serve with your favorite sides for a complete meal.

FOR STIR-FRY SAUCE:

1 cup (240 ml) chicken broth

¼ cup (62.5 g) hoisin sauce

2 tablespoons (30 ml) soy sauce

2 teaspoons sesame oil

1 tablespoon (8 g) cornstarch

FOR SHRIMP STIR-FRY:

2 tablespoons (30 ml) vegetable oil, divided

1 red bell pepper, cut into 2-inch (5 cm) slices

1 yellow bell pepper, cut into 2-inch (5 cm) slices

1 orange bell pepper, cut into 2-inch (5 cm) slices

½ yellow onion, cut into 2-inch (5 cm) strips

3 cups (210 g) broccoli florets

1 to 2 tablespoons (14 to 28 g) unsalted butter

Salt and ground black pepper

1½ teaspoons garlic paste

1 teaspoon ginger paste

1 pound (454 g) medium-size shrimp, peeled and deveined

Sliced scallion for garnish

Sesame seeds for garnish

1. To make the stir-fry sauce: In a medium-size bowl, whisk all the sauce ingredients until combined. Set aside.

2. Bring the griddle to medium-low heat.

3. To make the shrimp stir-fry: Pour 1 tablespoon (15 ml) of vegetable oil onto the griddle and place the bell peppers, onion, and broccoli in the oil. Add the butter and incorporate it into the vegetables. Season the vegetables with salt and pepper. Cook the vegetables for about 10 minutes, slowly mixing, or until the onion becomes translucent.

4. On another part of the griddle, combine 1 tablespoon (15 ml) of oil, the garlic paste, and ginger paste and mix to combine and cook until the garlic begins to brown (do not wait too long or the garlic will burn). Place the shrimp on the garlic-ginger mixture and cook, stirring, for 3 to 4 minutes, or until the shrimp are pink and opaque.

5. Mix the cooked shrimp with the vegetables. Pour in the stir-fry sauce a little at a time, using as much or as little sauce as you like. Serve garnished with the scallion and sesame seeds.

SHRIMP SCAMPI

SERVES 4

Brett introduced Adam to shrimp scampi, and it was an instant favorite! If you've never experienced the refreshing citrus explosion of shrimp scampi, this recipe will make you a forever fan, and the dinnertime hero!

4 ounces (115 g) angel hair pasta

2 tablespoons (30 ml) olive oil

4 tablespoons (½ stick, or 56 g) unsalted butter, divided

4 garlic cloves, minced

1 pound (454 g) fresh shrimp, peeled and deveined

¼ cup (60 ml) white wine

2 tablespoons (30 ml) freshly squeezed lemon juice

Salt and ground black pepper

¼ cup (16 g) chopped fresh parsley

1. Bring one side of the griddle to high heat.

2. Place a medium-size pot filled about three-fourths with water on the heat and bring to a boil. Add the pasta to the pot and stir. Cook according to the package directions.

3. While the pasta cooks, bring another section of the griddle to medium-low heat.

4. Once warm, pour the oil onto the griddle over medium-low heat and add 1 tablespoon (14 g) of butter to melt and the garlic. Once the butter melts, place the shrimp in the oil-butter mix and cook until all shrimp are nearly pink.

5. Pour the wine and lemon juice over the shrimp and season with 1 teaspoon of salt and 1 teaspoon of pepper, or to taste, and mix. Add the remaining 3 tablespoons (42 g) of butter and cook until the butter melts.

6. Drain the pasta. Place the pasta on the shrimp and cook for 1 minute while mixing it with the shrimp and sauce. Sprinkle with parsley to serve.

SHRIMP FRIED RICE

In the event that we have not been clear yet: We absolutely love fried rice! Pick your protein and the process is relatively the same. And the results? Perfection. Every. Time!

4 cups (800 g) jasmine rice

4 to 5 (60 to 75 ml) vegetable oil, divided, plus more as needed

8 tablespoons (1 stick, or 112 g) unsalted butter

3 to 4 tablespoons (45 to 60 ml) sweet soy sauce, plus more if needed

4 large eggs

1 (12-ounce, or 340 g) bag mixed frozen vegetables (corn, peas, carrots)

Sesame oil for cooking

2 garlic cloves, minced

1 pound (454 g) shrimp, peeled and deveined

Salt and ground black pepper

Sesame seeds for garnish

1. Cook the rice according to the package directions. Spread it out on a baking sheet and refrigerate, on the sheet, overnight to cool and dry.

2. Bring the griddle to medium-low heat.

3. Pour about 1 tablespoon (15 ml) of oil onto the griddle and place the butter in the oil to melt, followed by the rice. Cook the rice for 5 to 7 minutes, stirring and mixing. The rice will start to darken (slightly). Mix in the sweet soy sauce to taste.

4. On an open area of the heated griddle, pour on another 1 tablespoon (15 ml) of oil and crack the eggs into it. Once the eggs begin to cook, lightly scramble them for a minute or two, then mix the eggs into the rice and cook for 2 to 3 minutes more. Move the rice to the cooler section of the griddle, not over direct heat.

5. Pour another 1 to 2 tablespoons (15 to 30 ml) of oil onto the heated griddle and place the mixed vegetables in it. Season with sweet soy sauce to taste and a drizzle or two of sesame oil. Cook until the vegetables are hot and softened, then move the vegetables to the cooler side of the griddle and mix with the rice and eggs.

6. Because shrimp cook quickly, they are the last part of the cook. Pour the remaining 1 tablespoon (15 ml) of oil onto the griddle and put the garlic in it. Cook for 30 seconds until the garlic is fragrant and begins to brown. Lay the shrimp directly onto the garlic. Stir-fry for about 4 minutes until the shrimp are cooked through (they will turn a light pink color). Season the shrimp with sweet soy sauce to taste.

7. Bring the rice, eggs, and vegetables to the shrimp and mix everything together. Taste and season with salt and pepper, as needed, and garnish with a sprinkling of sesame seeds to serve.

CILANTRO LIME SHRIMP TACOS

SERVES 4

Brett takes the credit for this one. As a regular "taco night" favorite—its cool taste of the beach is refreshing on any hot, humid summer day—this recipe has made its appearance on griddle cooks dozens of times in the "backyard diner" and in Brett's "test kitchen." When you add this to your backyard diner, you can take all the credit! Waltwins tip: Before you add the raw shrimp, reserve some of the tasty marinade to pour over the cooked shrimp in the tacos.

Juice of 3 limes, plus a little extra

1 tablespoon (15 ml) olive oil

2 garlic cloves, minced

2 tablespoons (2 g) fresh cilantro, plus more for garnish

½ teaspoon ground cumin

1 pound (454 g) shrimp, peeled and deveined

8 to 10 (6-inch, or 15 cm) taco-size flour tortillas

1 (14-ounce, 395 g) bag coleslaw mix

Pico de gallo for serving

Creamy Jalapeño Ranch Dressing (see Chicken Street Tacos, page 71) for serving

1. In a medium-size bowl, whisk the juice of three limes, oil, garlic, cilantro, and cumin to combine. Add the shrimp and gently toss to coat in the marinade. Cover and refrigerate for 20 minutes—don't let it stay there too long, as the lime will begin to cook the shrimp.

2. Bring one side of the griddle to medium heat and let preheat for 5 minutes.

3. Remove half the shrimp from the marinade and place it on the heated side of the griddle. Cook for 3 minutes, or until the shrimp are pink on the bottom. Flip the shrimp and cook for 3 minutes more, or until the shrimp are completely pink. Move the cooked shrimp to the cooler side of the griddle, not over direct heat. Repeat with the remaining shrimp. Discard the marinade.

4. When all the shrimp are cooked, place the tortillas on the griddle for about 30 seconds, flipping, to warm.

5. Build the tacos: On each tortilla, place a layer of coleslaw mix, pico de gallo, and Creamy Jalapeño Ranch Dressing, then place four or five pieces of shrimp on top of the ranch. Garnish with a little more ranch and some cilantro.

BANG BANG SHRIMP

Do you have a favorite restaurant that has a food you crave regularly? This bang bang shrimp recipe was inspired by one of our favorite restaurants, Napolatanos in Gainesville, Florida, that, unfortunately, closed its doors. We made this version to bring back the many wonderful memories we had eating together at "Nappy's."

---

1 cup (240 g) mayonnaise

¾ cup (237 g) sweet chili sauce (Use liberally!)

2 teaspoons sriracha, plus more as needed

4 large eggs, beaten

3 to 4 cups (360 to 480 g) all-purpose flour

2 tablespoons (16 g) cornstarch

1 pound (454 g) shrimp, peeled and deveined

2 to 3 tablespoons (30 to 45 ml) vegetable oil, divided

1. In a large bowl, stir together the mayo, chili sauce, and sriracha until blended. Taste and add more sriracha, as needed. Set aside.

2. Place two shallow bowls side by side. Place the eggs in one bowl and stir together the flour and cornstarch in the other. Pat the shrimp dry with a paper towel. Coat the shrimp in the egg wash, then move it to the flour mixture to coat.

3. Bring the griddle to medium-low heat.

4. Pour the oil onto the griddle and let heat until you see a wisp of white smoke. Place the coated shrimp on the griddle in the hot shallow-fry oil. Cook the shrimp for 1 minute, or until the bottom is browned, turn, and repeat on the other side, adding more oil as needed. Transfer the cooked shrimp to the bowl with the sauce and stir to coat it evenly. Enjoy!

COCONUT SHRIMP

Do you love coconut? Do you love shrimp? Then this is the ultimate dish for you. Serve the coconut shrimp over Pineapple Coleslaw (page 42) in street-size (4½-inch, or 11 cm) flour tortillas for a real treat.

---

2 cups (480 ml) milk

2 large eggs

2 cups (240 g) all-purpose flour

2 cups (100 g) panko breadcrumbs

2 cups (240 g) sweetened coconut flakes

1 pound (454 g) medium-size shrimp, peeled and deveined

3 tablespoons (45 ml) vegetable oil

1. In a shallow bowl, whisk the milk and eggs to blend to create the wet dredge. Place the flour in another shallow bowl. In a large resealable plastic bag, combine the breadcrumbs and the coconut. Dry the shrimp and place them in the flour, then into the wet dredge. Once completely coated, place the shrimp in the breadcrumb-coconut mix. Seal the bag and gently turn to coat, ensuring all shrimp are completely covered with the coconut mix.

2. Bring the griddle to medium-low heat.

3. Pour the oil onto the griddle, creating a "puddle" shallow-fry area, and let heat until you see a wisp of white smoke. Place the coated shrimp in the hot oil and cook for 1 to 2 minutes until the bottom is golden. Flip the shrimp and cook for 1 to 2 minutes on the other side until golden.

SIZZLING SEA SCALLOPS

There may not be a more savory dish, or an easier dish, in this entire book than these sea scallops—and we're okay with that. The flavor profile is strong with this one.

¼ cup (60 ml) olive oil

1 pound (454 g) fresh sea scallops

1 tablespoon (18 g) salt

2 teaspoons ground black pepper

5 tablespoons (70 g) unsalted butter

3 garlic cloves, minced

¼ cup (16 g) chopped fresh parsley

1. Bring the griddle to medium to medium-high heat.

2. Pour the oil onto the griddle and let heat until you see a wisp of white smoke. Add the butter and garlic and let the butter melt and the garlic cook for 20 to 30 seconds until fragrant and light brown.

3. Season one side of the scallops with half of the salt and pepper and lay them in the oil-butter-garlic mixture, seasoned-side down. They should sizzle immediately. Season again with the remaining salt and pepper and cook for about 3 minutes until that first side is well seared and golden brown. Starting with the first scallop you placed on the griddle, flip them all. Cook for about 2 minutes more until golden and cooked through, then pull the scallops off the griddle, scooping up some of the melted butter and garlic to drizzle on top. Let rest for 3 minutes before serving garnished with parsley.

MAHI MAHI TACOS

Mahi mahi lives in saltwater habitats all over the world. But because fish supplies vary by season and location, you might need to substitute. For that, some good choices are tuna, cod, tilapia, and halibut.

---

1 pound (454 g) mahi mahi fillet,
    preferably about 1 to 1½ inches
    (2.5 to 3.8 cm) thick

Mahi Mahi Marinade (page 161)

1 tablespoon olive oil

4 soft taco shells

1 cup (240 g) coleslaw

1 lemon, quartered

2 teaspoons salt

2 teaspoons pepper

Pico de gallo or other
    tomato-based salsa

½ cup (60 g) Cotija cheese

½ cup (60 g) Waltwins Crema Sauce
    (page 161)

1. Place the mahi mahi in the prepared marinade and place in the refrigerator to chill for at least 30 minutes and, preferably, up to 3 or 4 hours.

2. Turn the griddle to medium heat. Once to temperature, pour the olive oil on the griddle, followed by the mahi mahi. Let cook for 3 minutes, and then flip and cook for an additional 3 minutes.

3. Remove from the heat and cut up into bite-sized pieces. Build a taco in a soft taco shell by placing down a bed of coleslaw, then placing the mahi mahi on the coleslaw. Squeeze fresh lemon juice on the fish, then add ½ teaspoon each of salt and pepper. Top with pico de gallo, sprinkle on Cotija cheese and a drizzle of crema sauce (as much as desired), and repeat with the other three tacos. Serve and enjoy!

WALTWINS CREMA SAUCE

15 OUNCES (425 G)

We created this crema specifically for our mahi mahi tacos. Little did we know this would be a favorite topper for many Mexican-style dishes. This is where we really started to appreciate the power of a little chipotle powder.

1 (15-ounce, or 425 g) container Mexican-style crema

Juice of 1 lemon or lime

1 teaspoon salt

1 teaspoon chipotle powder

1 teaspoon garlic powder

In a medium-size bowl, stir together all the ingredients (add the seasonings to taste) until evenly mixed. Cover and refrigerate to chill for at least 2 hours before serving.

MAHI MAHI MARINADE

MAKES ENOUGH TO COAT 2 MAHI MAHI FILLETS, OR OTHER FAVORITE FISH

From the first time Adam and Brett had a taste of fish tacos, they have always stood out as a "dark horse" fresh cook favorite. Making this marinade for our mahi mahi tacos means we can quickly cook crave-worthy fish tacos any time.

Juice of 2 lemons

2 teaspoons chipotle powder

2 teaspoons onion powder

2 teaspoons garlic powder

2 teaspoons salt

In a medium-size bowl, stir together all the ingredients (add the seasonings to taste) until evenly mixed.

SALMON PICCATA

Outdoor griddle cooking was made for fish cooks. Light and refreshing, this quick and simple cook is sure to please. Serve with your favorite pasta or side dish.

---

2 tablespoons (30 ml) olive oil

2 (8-ounce, or 225 g each) skinned
    salmon fillets

2 teaspoons salt

2 teaspoons ground black pepper

4 tablespoons (½ stick, or 56 g)
    unsalted butter

3 garlic cloves, minced

3 lemons, 1 halved, 1 cut into slices,
    1 quartered

1 to 2 tablespoons (9 to 18 g)
    capers, drained

¼ cup (16 g) fresh parsley

1. Bring the griddle to medium-low heat.

2. Pour the oil onto the griddle and let heat until you see a wisp of white smoke. Place the salmon fillets in the hot oil (you should hear the sizzle!). Season the top side of the salmon with half of the salt and half of the pepper. Cook for 2 to 3 minutes until you see a "white" line cooking up from the bottom of the fillets, until just shy of the halfway point.

3. Flip the fillets and place the butter and garlic onto the griddle surface. Season the fillets with the remaining salt and pepper. Squeeze both lemon halves over the fillets, then cover them with the capers and lemon slices. Cook for 2 to 3 minutes more, basting with the garlic butter, until the salmon is cooked all the way through (it will be light pink in color) and flakes easily with a fork.

4. Pull the salmon off the griddle and let rest for 2 to 3 minutes. Garnish with parsley and serve with lemon quarters for squeezing.

FISH & CHIPS

There are a few dishes that, once we began to cook regularly, we both knew we wanted to master. Although we may not have "mastered" this one just yet, this recipe for fish and chips is exactly what we hoped it would be. These few ingredients take your fish-fry cook to the next level.

FOR TARTAR SAUCE:

1 cup (240 g) mayonnaise

1 cup (245 g) dill pickle relish, or (150 g) finely chopped dill pickle, plus more as needed

1 tablespoon (4 g) fresh dill

1½ teaspoons freshly squeezed lemon juice, plus more as needed

1 teaspoon sugar

¼ teaspoon ground black pepper

1 tablespoon (7 g) onion powder, plus more as needed

FOR FISH AND CHIPS:

1½ cups (180 g) all-purpose flour, divided

½ cup (64 g) cornstarch, divided

1 teaspoon baking powder

1½ teaspoons salt

1 cup (240 ml) club soda

1 tablespoon (12 g) Waltwins Usual Suspects Seasoning (page 52)

6 tablespoons (90 ml) peanut oil or other oil of choice, divided

1½ pounds (681 g) fresh cod, cut to your desired size

2 large potatoes, cut into french fry strips

Salt and ground black pepper

Malt vinegar for serving

1. To make the tartar sauce: In a medium-size bowl, whisk all the sauce ingredients until evenly mixed. Add more relish, lemon juice, or onion powder to taste. Cover and refrigerate until serving.

2. To make the fish: In a medium-size bowl, stir together 1 cup (120 g) of flour, ¼ cup (32 g) of cornstarch, the baking powder, and salt. Stir in enough club soda to make a batter about the consistency of a thin pancake batter. Season the batter to taste with the Usual Suspects Seasoning. Set aside.

3. In another medium-size bowl, stir together the remaining ½ cup (60 g) of flour and ¼ cup (32 g) of cornstarch.

4. Bring the griddle to medium-low heat.

5. Pour 3 tablespoons (45 ml) of oil onto the griddle and let heat for 3 to 5 minutes. You want to create a "shallow-fry" by keeping the oil in one area on the griddle.

6. Dredge the fish in the dry flour-cornstarch mixture. Shake off any excess. Dip the dredged fish into the batter, letting any excess drip off before carefully placing the fish on the hot griddle. Cook the fish until golden brown on both sides and it flakes easily with a fork. Transfer to paper towels to drain. Keep warm.

7. To make the chips: Fill a large bowl with ice and water. Set aside. Bring a medium-large saucepan full of water to a boil. Add the fries and boil for 5 minutes. Immediately transfer the fries to the ice bath to stop the cooking process.

8. Bring an area of the griddle to medium-high heat.

9. Pour the remaining 3 tablespoons (45 ml) of oil onto the medium-high heat area to create another shallow-fry setup. Let the oil heat for 3 to 5 minutes. Carefully place the potatoes in the hot oil and cook, turning constantly, until they are golden brown. Transfer the fries to a cooling rack on the griddle, but away from the heat to keep warm, and place a dome over the fries to cook them a bit more. Once they are cooked to your desired crispiness, serve the fish and fries with the tartar sauce and malt vinegar.

SEARED AHI TUNA

Ahi tuna is another favorite of Brett's that is perfect for the griddle! If you need the ultimate savory yet light dish, this one delivers! This is another weekly go-to at Brett's home!

2 fresh tuna steaks

2 tablespoons (30 ml) soy sauce

1½ teaspoons sesame oil

1 to 2 tablespoons (8 to 16 g) black and white sesame seeds, mixed

2 tablespoons (30 ml) olive oil

1. Pat the tuna steaks completely dry with a paper towel. In a small bowl or on a small plate, stir together the soy sauce and sesame oil. Pour the sesame seeds onto another small plate. Place the tuna in the soy–sesame oil mixture and ensure it is completely coated. Then lay it in the sesame seeds and press lightly to help cover the entire backside of the tuna with seeds. Flip and do the same to the other side. Roll the sides in the seeds to completely cover the tuna in sesame seeds.

2. Bring the griddle to high heat.

3. Pour the olive oil onto the griddle and place the tuna in the oil. Cook for 1 minute per side. Pull the tuna off the griddle and let rest for 5 to 10 minutes before serving. Cut the tuna against the grain into slices to serve.

ABOUT THE AUTHORS

Adam and Brett Walton have always had a passion for cooking. Their sister, Angie, shared the same passion and would share her ideas with the twins. Being identical twins put Adam and Brett in the spotlight often, and they became natural performers. This led them to create their WALTWINS YouTube Channel in 2017. Although the channel struggled to find footing in a specific niche for the first two and a half years, their passion for cooking would, ultimately, drive them to change their fast-food review channel into an outdoor griddle cooking channel in March 2020. Little did they know that this change would alter the trajectory of both their channel and their lives. On August 14, 2020, they were named YouTube's "Creator on the Rise" and were honored to have landed on YouTube's recommended page, where six of their griddle cooks were featured for the whole day. In June 2021, they used their WALTWINS YouTube Channel to create an official brand and business in Central Florida, where they have begun planning for future growth and exciting developments.

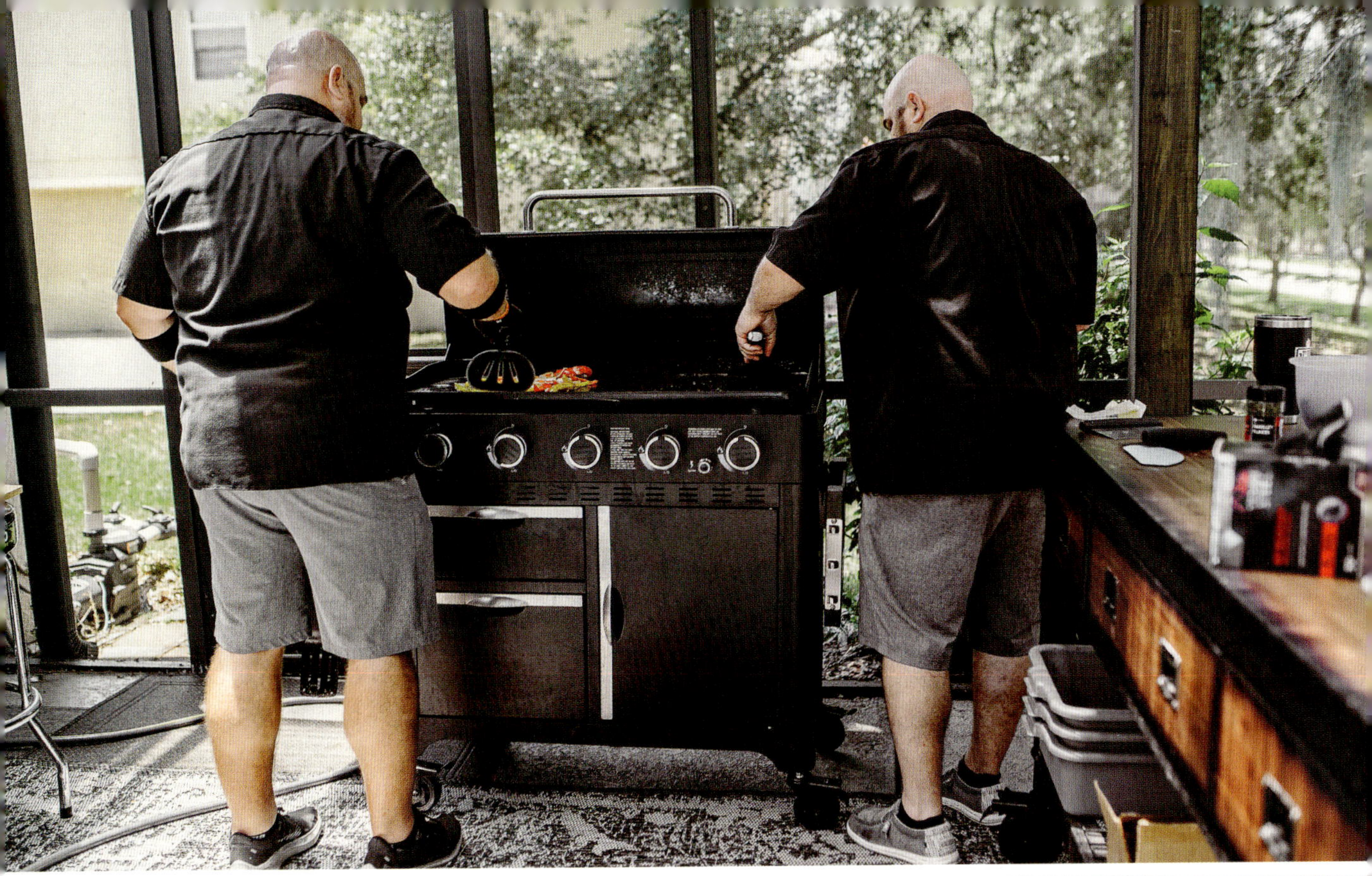
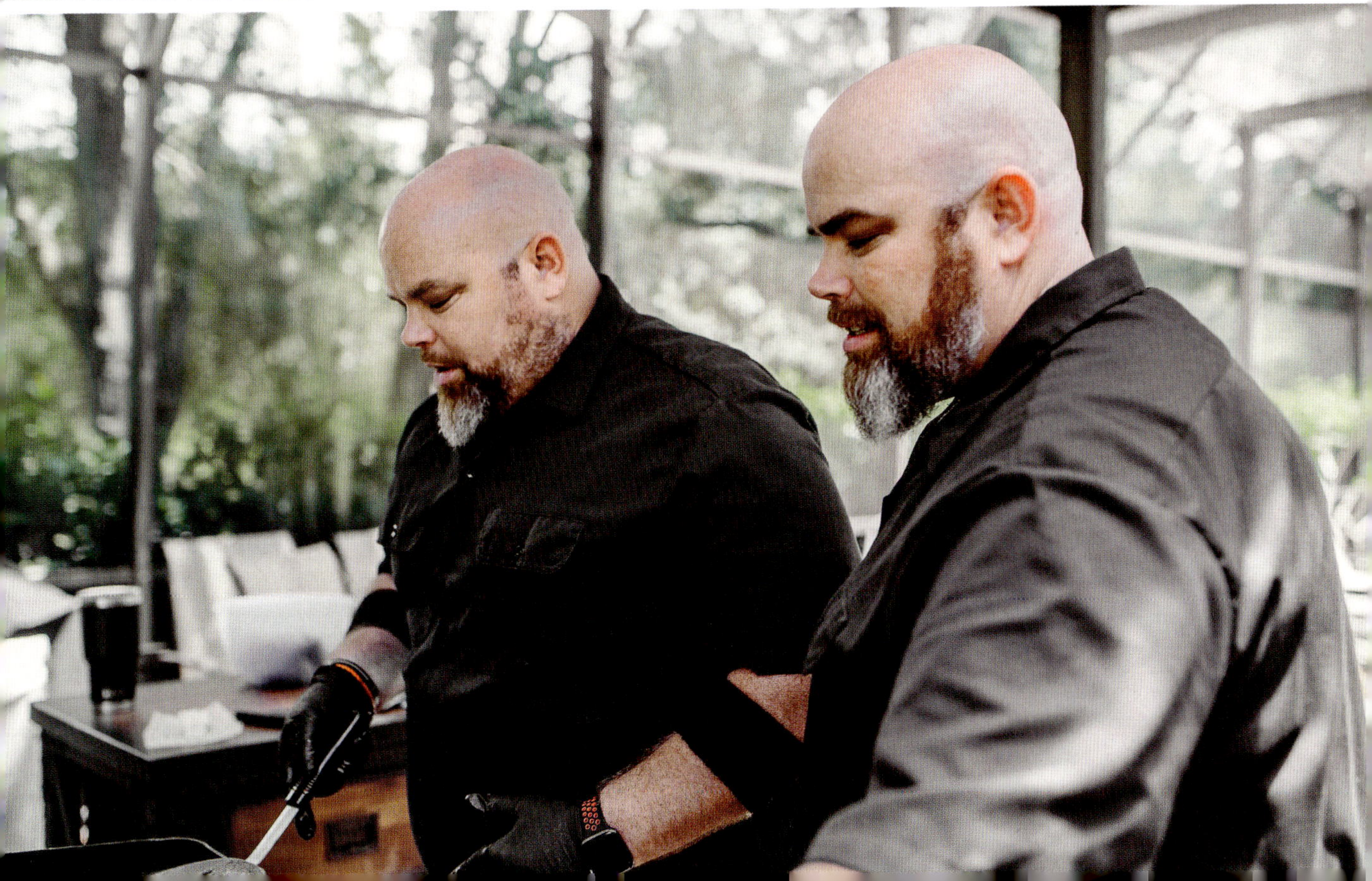

ACKNOWLEDGMENTS

We are so thankful to the many people who have helped our dreams become a reality! First, we know we would not be able to do what we do without the direct support of our families: Adam's wife, Jennifer Walton; and their children Kenzie, Cannon, Parker, and Griffin; and Brett's girlfriend, Sherry Sheffield, and his daughters Brittany and Angie.

We also have to thank our dad, John Walton, for always believing in us, no matter what we were doing. His positivity has been a driving force in our lives that continues to impact us daily. Our mom, Melinda Walton, instilled a love of good home cooking, and our sister, Angela Grimmer, inspired us to create amazing dishes—and is still the best cook we know! Coming from a large family, everyone has had a hand in helping raise us and in inspiring us in different ways. Our sister Marcy has always been a stalwart of confidence, and she and our little sis Molly have been constant cheerleaders, whatever we were doing. Tad and Jennie were there to offer timely support when we were younger.

Mikela Rodriguez was instrumental in helping us drive our YouTube channel into an official brand and business, and she has guided us throughout the recipe-creation process. We also recognize that the opportunity to create a cookbook would have never come to fruition without the amazing audience that has supported us on YouTube and other social media platforms and throughout our griddle-cooking journey. Thank you!

Gerald and Margarita Beebe have always been supportive and offered quick and meaningful advice. Thanks to Joy Glanzer for also always believing in us and for being the greatest aunt anyone could have! We would be remiss if we did not recognize that without the vision of Dan Rosenberg, we would have never even hoped to create a griddle cookbook. Thank you for reaching out, Dan! We thank our friend and photographer, Colleen Hillard, for doing an incredible job of making our food come to life, and Leigh Olson, for her amazing photos, too.

Within the cooking community, there are so many who have come into our lives and have made a meaningful impact. These include Todd Toven, Desirèe "Blackstone Betty" Dukes, Chef Nathan Lippy, CJ Frazier, Wade Williams, Justin "CJ" Volkmann, Thomas Scarano, Matthew Arbaszewski, Barrett Browne, Matthew Hussey, Neal Williams, Kent "Daddy Dutch" Vandeweerd, Steve Brown, Butch Bennett, The Griddle Guys, and Maddi and Kiki Longo.

INDEX